Learning Not Schooling

Reimagining the Purpose of Education

Lyn Lesch

Rowman & Littlefield Education
Lanham • New York • Toronto • Plymouth, UK

Published in the United States of America
by Rowman & Littlefield Education
A Division of Rowman & Littlefield Publishers, Inc.
A wholly owned subsidiary of The Rowman & Littlefield Publishing Group,
Inc.
4501 Forbes Boulevard, Suite 200, Lanham, Maryland 20706
www.rowmaneducation.com

Estover Road
Plymouth PL6 7PY
United Kingdom

Copyright © 2009 by Lyn Lesch

British Library Cataloguing in Publication Information Available

Library of Congress Cataloging-in-Publication Data

Lesch, Lyn, 1948–
  Learning not schooling: reimagining the purpose of education / Lyn Lesch.
     p. cm.
  Includes bibliographical references.
  ISBN-13: 978-1-60709-097-7 (cloth: alk. paper)
  ISBN-10: 1-60709-097-X (cloth: alk. paper)
  ISBN-13: 978-1-60709-098-4 (pbk.: alk. paper)
  ISBN-10: 1-60709-098-8 (pbk.: alk. paper)
  ISBN-13: 978-1-60709-099-1 (e-book)
  ISBN-10: 1-60709-099-6 (e-book)
  1. Education—Aims and objectives—United States. 2. Educational change—
United States. I. Title.
  LA210.L465 2009
  370.10973—dc22   2008050125

™ The paper used in this publication meets the minimum requirements of
American National Standard for Information Sciences—Permanence of Paper
for Printed Library Materials, ANSI/NISO Z39.48-1992.
Manufactured in the United States of America.

Contents

Acknowledgments

I am grateful to my editor at Rowman & Littlefield Education, Tom Koerner, for his thoughtful suggestions concerning all three of my books, including this one. I am also grateful to those parents and students at The Children's School in Evanston, Illinois, who helped broaden my horizons concerning both child development and learning. I am likewise indebted to both Bill Pollack and Jim Wasner for all the discussions I have had with both of them over the years about education, human development, and related matters. Most of all, though, I am indebted to my brother Chip and my sister-in-law Sheryl, without whose continued support and encouragement over the years neither my school nor my writings in education would have been possible.

Introduction

One tends to repeatedly hear the same frustrations and hand-wringing over the state of contemporary education. American students are not keeping pace with their chronological peers in other countries, particularly in light of the present global economy; there are enormous inequities between the education which students receive in affluent neighborhoods and that which those students who attend schools in the hard-core inner city receive; test scores in various schools are slipping despite the added funding that those schools have received.

Authors such as Jonathan Kozol go on writing well-intentioned, passionate books on the subject of the inequities between rich and poor in regard to educational opportunity, with very little change ever occurring. Political debates, particularly in years in which there is an election of a new president, resonate with the very same discussions of how American education is failing its students, this assessment being invariably determined by scores on standardized tests. And our fear of other countries in the present global economy, such as China and India, leaving the United States behind is inevitably tied to the failure of our schools to educate students in certain critical areas such as math and science.

In fact, it is highly possible that these same discussions have reached the point where, because they are made over and over again in the very same manner by people in similar positions, the American public may be on the verge of tuning them out simply because we have heard them all so many times before. Consequently, people may be already beginning to lose faith in the idea that our educational system can indeed be significantly reformed so that better schools are created.

Indeed, it is quite possible that teachers, administrators, and other educators, because they have often heard themselves cast as villains in our ongoing national discussion about education, one in which the particulars of the analysis never seem to change, may themselves begin to lose hope in what can actually be done to change things. Combine this despair with the sheer fact that the particular system in which these professionals labor each day is itself often a significant impediment to their primary goal of educating their students, and one begins to get a true glimpse of the magnitude of the problem.

Yet, strangely enough, despite all the frustration and despair, nearly all the discussions about contemporary education in this country which are now taking place seem to concern the possible attempt to reform schools as they now stand. Seldom do serious discussions take place concerning what effective learning is and how that process may or may not be tied to the process of schooling. For learning and schooling may be not only entirely different endeavors. It is also possible that the latter may on occasion be an actual impediment to the former.

That is to say, it is conceivable that our attempt to school students in their formative years may actually be leading them in a direction within themselves that is contrary to their own natural, inquisitive nature. And if that is in fact the case, then the answers to changing contemporary schooling for the better might lie not necessarily with reforming it but with scrapping the present idea of it altogether in favor of an approach toward learning that is more in sync with the natural tendencies of the learner.

For if students are being schooled in a manner that causes the process of learning to become unnatural, the primary difficulty lies with the entire structure of schooling itself, not with certain inadequacies that are part of that structure. To pay teachers more money and in so doing attempt to attract more talented individuals to the profession; or to make both students and teachers more accountable for learning by consistently testing the students to be certain that certain standards are being met; or even to reduce the number of students whom the average classroom teacher is responsible for educating then become only stopgap measures aimed at fixing a system which inevitably works directly against the natural tendencies of the learner.

Unfortunately, this rather obvious question concerning what the basic, intrinsic relationship is between learning and schooling is not only not now part of our national discussion. It rarely comes up at all. Rather, what is referred to incessantly is how to better structure our schools so that empirical validations of learning, which are part of the current national testing program, can be brought up to speed, so to speak. In other words, it is the results of schooling which are usually examined rather than the actual process of learning itself.

In addition, what are also being unfortunately and significantly left out of our national discussion are questions concerning the possible relationship, or lack thereof, between empirical standards and the actual abilities which those standards are designed to measure. Also being significantly ignored is a more careful examination of race, culture, and socioeconomics as they pertain to the use of test scores.

Although a number of books have certainly been written about this latter subject, they seem to invariably address issues such as how inner-city students are being inadequately prepared to perform well on such tests or occasionally about how the tests are affecting the personal development of these students in unhealthy ways. Seldom does one hear about the possibility that the existence of the tests themselves may be a well-disguised form of institutional prejudice aimed at keeping certain groupings in our society permanently disenfranchised.

Of course, significantly related to the possibility of changing the essential nature of learning in our society is the existence of the World Wide Web and how that might be employed so that students are given greater control over their learning rather than continue to simply be schooled by an educational system which appears to be significantly broken. In particular, the limitless interconnectedness which the Web affords us might be used to connect students in their formative years with experts from the world of work and higher education, people who have much greater access to the tools, knowledge, and information which young people will need to be successful in the future than do most classroom teachers and school administrators.

We have been wringing our hands for too long now about the same two important issues. The first has to do simply with how students in many schools are simply not learning as well as they might. The second has to do with the inequities that exist in our schools between the rich and the poor. Therefore, what appears to be called for is an entirely new model, one that addresses the issue of what healthy, effective learning is and does not necessarily connect such learning to the process of schooling as it now stands.

A recent candidate for president of the United States put forth the idea that the Department of Education, as it now stands, has reached the point where it has become an unnecessary albatross that needs to be eliminated. As shocking as such language might initially be for many parents and educators, the idea behind it may in fact be an essentially sound one. For to significantly change how students in our society learn, not how effectively they are schooled but how successfully they learn, it seems that we may indeed have to begin by eliminating those institutional structures which impede such an effort.

So, the answer to the two significant issues that continue to trouble us, learning in young people that often doesn't reach its full potential and inequities in our educational system between members of different racial and socioeconomic groupings, may indeed lie in a different approach to both learning and schooling, one in which learning and the opportunities that learning brings lie essentially in the hands of the learner himself.

Ivan Illich published his classic book *Deschooling Society* nearly forty years ago. In it, he wrote of how the essential question in education might not necessarily be what should someone learn, although that is of course significant, but instead, what kinds of things might learners want to be in contact with in order that they *can* learn?

What might well make a difference is to begin to think of schools more in terms of how they can be used to effectively connect students to the larger society into which they are headed so that their learning becomes more of a personal activity, rather than continuing to perceive schooling as the ability to demonstrate, through certain empirical validations, that one has acquired the skills, knowledge, and information which one is taught inside the typical self-contained classroom. To this end, the question that might become uppermost in the minds of young people could be: how can I best use what is available to me, particularly in the world that exists outside the schoolhouse door, to acquire all those things that will allow me to become a successful person?

However, this probably won't occur unless we significantly expand the concept of what a good education for young people entails; unless we begin to give up the idea that classroom teachers and other professional educators should have the sort of exclusive role that they now have in what information and knowledge students acquire; and, as much as anything, unless we begin to give up the notion that learning and schooling are necessarily coincidental.

There is indeed a healthier model available to us, one that might well begin to transcend the often false promise of traditional education. Yet this new model, which is the subject of this work, might have no chance of being effectively put in place unless we begin to move toward a more deschooled society, one in which the field of opportunities for learning is significantly expanded outward into the world that our students in their formative years will one day inhabit.

It may well be that the reason that many of our schools have in the past been unsuccessful is simply because they are working at cross purposes to the natural inquisitive nature of human beings rather than being coincidental with it. To this end, then, an appropriate starting point for a discussion of how to make learning, rather than schooling, the fulcrum of our educational system might lie in examining the ways in which learning and schooling might be inherently different processes.

Chapter One

Learning and Schooling

Carl Rogers, in his classic book *Freedom to Learn for the 80s*, drawing on his experience of studying moths when he was a young boy, wrote of how he essentially created, exclusively out of his curiosity about the subject, a laboratory for learning about moths in the fields of his family's farm.

This meant finding a book which allowed him to study how caterpillars become butterflies, learning how to feed baby caterpillars, learning how to keep and sustain caterpillars through a whole series of life changes, and then learning not only how to feed the cocoons from the right varieties of trees but also how to keep the cocoons alive in winter so that they didn't dry out. In other words, Rogers's open-ended explorations brought him increasingly in touch with the ecological balance that exists between the natural world and the creatures that inhabit it.

Similarly, there is a marvelous account in, of all places, Henry Miller's *Tropic of Capricorn* which depicts the same sort of self-initiated, unpredictable learning by Miller and a group of his boyhood friends. Having all just become avid readers, they would stand in a certain vacant lot, which had become their anointed meeting place, roasting chippies over an open fire and eagerly discussing whatever fascinating subject one of them had recently discovered.

These subjects concerned such things as the ancient Egyptians' knowledge of blood circulating through the body, the Japanese Current, burial rights and ceremonies in various parts of the world, cannibalism, the Aztecs, the buffaloes dying out, strange diseases, wizardry, the formation of precious stones, ghosts and the possible transmigration of souls, rubber plantations, various methods of torture, or what it might be like to stand on the moon.

In the same vein, I can remember a discussion that took place at my school in Evanston, Illinois, one day when an extremely bright thirteen-year-old girl, who had become interested in what three twelve-year-old boys had been learning about theoretical physics, struggled with Einstein's idea of special relativity. This is his theory that events that occur at the same time are seen at different times by two people who are in different locations simply because the speed of light never speeds up or slows down to accommodate itself to our perceptions.

Watching her standing at the blackboard, intently drawing diagrams of her own creation to try to convince me and one of the boys who was trying to explain the idea of relativity to her that the theory didn't make sense, it was easy to recognize that, despite the girl's frustration, this was actively engaged learning in its purest form. That is, this was the case of a learner coming to a subject entirely on her own, out of her intense desire to understand the apparent uniqueness of it, while at the same time not being at all sure where this new world of understanding she was now entering might eventually take her.

In looking more closely at these three examples of learning in which the curiosities of the learner were being thoroughly engaged, it seems rather obvious that one has to then indeed ask the question: what specific characteristics might all three situations share? The answer seems to be quite obvious. All three are examples of acquaintances with specific areas of knowledge that proceeded in a manner which is both self-initiated and unpredictable. That is, in all three cases, learners became acquainted with areas of interest which they themselves had chosen to consider, and their continued engagement with these areas took place in an entirely unpredictable manner.

Just as importantly, the curiosity and energy that fueled the learning process in each of these cases transpired exactly because they were self-chosen, unpredictable encounters with certain aspects of these young people's worlds. Carl Rogers set off to explore his family farm and found himself drawn toward an unexpected interest in moths and butterflies. Henry Miller and his pals were open to whatever one of them had just read that interested the group as a whole, even though their investigations took place entirely in a vacant lot in Brooklyn.

The thirteen-year-old girl at my school who became suddenly interested in the ideas inherent in special relativity did so completely unexpectedly one day as she listened to the twelve-year-old boys discuss how the ever-constant speed of light may affect when different observers apprehend different events. In addition, her investigations at the blackboard took place with such intensity largely because she had now entered a world of time and space that was entirely different from any that she had previously thought existed.

From the other side of the spectrum, Herbert Kohl, in his classic book about non-learning *I Won't Learn from You*, discusses his refusal as a boy to learn Yiddish simply because he didn't want to be party to conversations which excluded his mother, who couldn't speak it. From there, he goes on to discuss how certain young people he has known, many who were members of certain minority racial or socioeconomic groupings, refused to learn certain subjects or skills as a means of holding onto their unique identities and their dignity.

Along the same lines, I can remember one nine-year-old girl whom I taught who essentially refused to learn mathematics in the face of parental pressure to do so for essentially the same reason, that is, out of an attempt to assert her independent stature with them.

I mention these examples of learning that is either propelled by intense curiosity that is left alone to flourish or else is intentionally rebuffed for reasons of personal dignity in order to make a point. This is simply that if we are to provide a system for engendering the most natural learning in young people, we are going to have to make more of an effort, as Carl Rogers suggested, to get inside the minds of young people who are learning various subject matter and to better understand the relevant personal dynamics.

In examining such dynamics, it would seem that, as is exemplified in the case of Rogers setting up a laboratory of his own creation in order to study moths on his family farm or with Henry Miller standing in a back lot with his friends, eagerly discussing what someone had just discovered concerning wizardry or the Japanese Current, there is an important element that needs to be kept completely out of the learning process if it is to remain pure. That element is, of course, predetermined outcomes conceived by someone other than the learner himself.

Jean Piaget found that young people learn through a process of assimilation and accommodation by which they assimilate new conceptions of their world into already formed cognitive structures. However, as anyone who has studied his observations of children knows, he also found that this process cannot fully take place unless the child is able to in effect reconstruct the particulars of his world by discovering them for himself, that is, by ceaselessly attempting to find a way to assimilate new facts and ideas into the logic of what he already knows to be true.

This means that learning, by its very nature, must be an active, organic, and open-ended process. Otherwise, if the learner is subjected to instruction that is based on preconceived repetition, he is not himself actively engaged in creating a clearer conception of his world based on what he has previously learned. Rather, he is mechanically taking in new facts, information, or skills, often without fully understanding them.

Furthermore, meaningful learning, more than many of us realize, tends to proceed in this very same manner in which Piaget envisioned it. That is, young people often absorb important ideas and information about their world only when they are allowed to determine for themselves the direction of their learning and when they are permitted to remain curious about what they will encounter just around the next corner.

Therefore, it is being proposed here that the best learning experiences are those in which the learner himself chooses what he wants to investigate yet, at the same time, doesn't know where his investigations will necessarily lead. Like the pure explorations of Carl Rogers or Henry Miller and his schoolboy chums, because these explorations are undertaken merely to comprehend some aspect of one's world with which one wants to be in touch, they lead increasingly outward into that world. That is, each keeps expanding into something larger, fueled only by the curiosity of the learner.

Contrast this type of learning, which takes place purely and naturally, with the sort of preprogrammed instruction which takes place in most classrooms today, and one begins to get a true sense of the size of the problem. John Holt, in one of his classic books from the 1960s *How Children Fail*, wrote of the frustration of a colleague at the school where he taught, who told Holt one day, "I teach, but they don't learn." After considering the question of why so many students don't learn what they are taught, something which he struggled to answer for years, Holt said that the answer he eventually found boils down to one essential thing: often students don't learn exactly *because* we teach them. That is, we try to control the contents of their minds.

This rather striking example may be an indicator that points toward the possibility that not only is optimal learning and schooling not necessarily the same thing, but also the latter may often be an actual impediment to the former. More specifically, this supposition might be true, as much as anywhere, in John Holt's assertion that attempting to control the contents of young people's minds often causes them to be unable to learn. Yet, why might this be so?

One answer might be because the idea of schooling itself in which a set curriculum, often separated into prepackaged units and introduced by a teacher in order to achieve a predetermined result, is in essence diametrically opposed to how healthy learning evolves. That is, the structure of many schools themselves may, by their very nature, actually impede and stifle how learning tends to proceed naturally, if allowed to do so.

Of course, it is absolutely necessary that learners pursue subject matter sequentially so that they can clearly absorb it. The difficulty, however, often seems to come when the particular sequence which they are following is chosen for them by their teacher, who often sits in judgment of how well they have learned. For then, the manner that genuine learning tends to naturally proceed is often subverted. That is, it is no longer chosen by the learner, and its outcomes are no longer open-ended and unpredictable. In other words, increasingly preconceived curriculums, put in place to produce certain external results on standardized tests, are the real villains here.

In addition, there may be another essential reason why schooling as it now stands tends to hinder optimal learning. This is that it exists, in most cases, entirely within the closed system of the self-contained classroom. That is, if young people's learning is to remain pure, it must not be constrained by unnatural boundaries which impede its forward movement. Whereas, the manner in which young people are usually schooled in our society presupposes the existence of an inherent dividing line which separates what occurs inside schools from what transpires in the world outside them.

So, as a consequence of this, this line of demarcation between classrooms and the society in which they exist then tends to block the natural sequence of many learning progressions. Primarily, what is being referred to here is the lack of connection between schools and the world of adult expertise from which students could learn, which surrounds them.

John Dewey, in his classic book *Democracy and Education*, wrote of how when subject matter does not carry forward the natural impulses and curiosities of the learner to significant fruition, then the particular subject becomes just something to be learned in school rather than something that possesses a genuine reason to be acquired in and of itself. This is really at the heart of why learning progressions that never leave the schoolhouse door eventually double back upon themselves for young people as just "something that one has to learn." As a result, all of the same frustrations which one sees in so many students and teachers today come to fruition all over again.

It has become fashionable recently, particularly with the decoding of the human genome, to look at knowledge almost as something that occurs organically in the brain rather than looking at it, as Piaget did, as something that young people create by building it themselves out of a unique process of trial and error. Increasingly, many geneticists and learning theorists are viewing knowledge almost as an intrinsic property of the brain rather than as something that is organically constructed by those who come to it.

In addition, of course, with the recent introduction of the personal computer and Internet into education and schooling, cognitive learning has tended to become more preconceived and preprogrammed than ever. Yes, of course, young people have a greater opportunity to create their knowledge of their world by merely surfing the Web. Yet, the sort of preprogrammed instruction found today in many schools, even in many of the homeschooling-based online charter schools which currently exist, tends, it would seem, to work in opposition to what Piaget discovered concerning how children have the capacity to organically create a well-organized conception of their world.

It may well be that many of the difficulties which we have experienced in developing a workable education system have to do simply with the fact that the systems and methods we have created run so contrary to how learning naturally occurs within all of us, particularly in young people.

Consequently, if such is indeed the case, we may need to begin not by necessarily discussing what the essential structure of adequate schooling might be so that we can change it for the better. Rather, we might have to begin by examining how the process of learning evolves naturally in any learner and then work outward from there toward asking ourselves what sort of educational system might reflect this process. Almost certainly, we need to in fact try to make schooling the outcome of the most natural learning, to which people such as Carl Rogers and Henry Miller have alluded.

There may indeed be a way for young people's learning to proceed both naturally and sequentially, which is very much at the center of what this book is all about and will, consequently, be addressed from different angles in the chapters which follow. Suffice it to say here that we might be well served to begin with examinations of how grades, test scores, and other externally driven evaluations of learning might stifle initiative and with how narrowly defined subject matter might impede curiosity.

Chapter Two

Grades, Tests, and Initiative

How well do grades, test scores, and other purely empirical measures of ability accurately reflect what they are endeavoring to measure? More specifically, what is the exact relationship between these two things? That is, can one's knowledge of and skill level in a particular learning area be determined by a test score that does not measure the process by which a particular student's abilities were acquired? Furthermore, do grades and standardized test scores ever measure a student's capacity to take what he has learned in an academic situation and then apply it in the real world that lies outside it?

The school I founded and directed in Evanston did not give grades, and we did not, as a matter of course, employ any sort of standardized testing. However, occasionally when students who were leaving our school to go to high school needed test scores in order to apply to the school for which they sought admission, we would use the Iowa Tests of Basic Skills (ITBS).

Because our school was very small, usually consisting of no more than twenty students, the teachers got to know the abilities of the young people in the school quite well. That is, we learned very specifically just what individual students were capable of in different academic areas. So when they were tested, it was obvious just how well their performance on the ITBS reflected their actual abilities.

What we found was that many of the students' test scores, although often being a fairly accurate representation of certain weak-
nesses they might possess in regard to highly specific academic
skills or knowledge, often didn't reflect their strengths, their potential, or their actual capabilities. I can think of one student who
learned advanced theoretical physics at age twelve but didn't score
significantly well on the science part of the ITBS because it dealt
with different areas in science that he hadn't really covered simply
because they seemed too basic and irrelevant to what he had a genuine interest in learning and was also capable of learning.

I can also remember students who learned fairly advanced algebra
and had even peeked over the perimeter of their studies into calculus but did not score high on the basic mathematics part of the test
that required them to solve problems within a certain period of time.
Because lessons at our school were never subjected to the sort of
time constraints that they often are in more traditional schools, our
students were at a distinct disadvantage when it came to this section
simply because the idea of solving problems within a narrow time
frame was something that was still exceedingly foreign to them.

These are just two examples of students' actual capabilities in certain academic areas not being accurately reflected by empirical test
scores. Both of them have to do with the tests' inability to take into
account all the relevant factors before assigning a specific score to a
rather wide area of learning. This means that, in both of the above
cases, there were a number of factors which lay outside not only the
particular field of information that the test was measuring but also
existed outside the manner in which students actually acquired certain information, knowledge, and skills.

In the case of the student who learned advanced physics and was
then able to employ that knowledge to learn more on his own about
the subject, the science part of the ITBS not only didn't measure an
area with which most students of a similar age would never have
been acquainted but also didn't measure the capacity of the student
to take this knowledge and then begin investigations on his own.

In the case of the students who were learning fairly advanced algebra and even calculus, the mathematics section of the test which dealt with how accurately students can solve problems in basic mathematics within a narrow time frame didn't take into account the actual process for learning mathematics to which students at our school had been exposed.

These two seemingly minor examples of how testing doesn't necessarily reflect learning are mentioned here for a reason. Each reflects what should be a significant area of concern for us all as far as how the process of testing in various academic areas might paint an incomplete picture of not only what students are actually capable but also of the effects which the particular learning process they employ might have on certain empirical validations of their abilities.

For if standardized test scores, particularly those which are part of the No Child Left Behind program, become increasingly the benchmark for how well students are learning and have the sort of pronounced effect on their future that they now do while there might be two significant variables that bear no relation to those scores, then, it seems, the current national testing program might need to be called even more into question than it already has been.

There will, of course, be those who argue that current standardized tests are implemented merely to ascertain whether or not students have been able to acquire highly specific capabilities. That is to say, they should not be required to measure either what students might be capable of outside the narrowly defined boundaries of the particular subject area they are designed to measure or the process by which students acquire certain abilities. And of course there is some truth to this argument.

However, it seems, there is a larger area of concern here. This is simply that if current standardized tests are used as a definition for successful learning as they increasingly are, and if both the capabilities of students which exist outside the scores on these tests and the particular process by which they acquire knowledge or skills are not given their full measure of attention, a rather erroneous picture of student learning is then being painted for the students, their teachers, and the public at large.

Then, in response to this erroneous picture, educators often begin a process of narrowing subject matter for students in accordance with this false picture in order to improve test scores. For example, a group of students scores poorly on a test which purports to measure their abilities in basic mathematics in a highly specific manner. However, their poor scores in large measure reflect the fact that because they have such a good grasp of many of the underlying concepts related to the test questions, they are able to see that many of the problems for which they are being asked to provide answers cannot realistically be solved in the sort of highly specific way which the test requires.

Consequently, in response to their lower test scores, their teacher, particularly because she feels pressure from the administration in her school to produce higher scores, begins to narrow the mathematics curriculum which she presents to her students. Therefore, as a result of this, because the test wasn't able to accurately measure the scope of understanding of mathematics by a number of students, a scope which was in fact much greater than the questions on the test itself, the students are now ironically being subjected to an even narrower approach to math, even though the initial approach being employed with them was probably too narrow in the first place.

It seems not much of a stretch to believe that this constriction of students' curriculum in different areas in response to test scores which inaccurately reflect their true abilities goes on in schools even more than many educators would like to admit. In addition, of course, not only are curricula often oversimplified, but teachers' willingness to trust their own perceptions of what their students are capable and to create the sort of curricula which truly challenge them might also be significantly undermined.

Jonathan Kozol, in the chapter in his recent book *The Shame of the Nation: The Restoration of Apartheid Schooling in America* which deals with the effects of standardized testing on inner-city students, quotes Deborah Meier, the award-winning, lifelong educator who founded pioneering schools in both New York City and Boston. Meier decries how the heavy reliance upon high-stakes testing in our schools has led many classroom teachers to distrust their own abilities to see and observe the children they are teaching and to derive valid conclusions based upon those observations.

Alfie Kohn, in his book *The Case against Standardized Testing*, makes the point that in younger children (i.e., students below fourth grade) many skills develop very rapidly and very differently, not necessarily following any kind of predictable timeline. Therefore, trying to measure different capacities of children in this age group is both unrealistic and unfruitful. Kohn goes on to make the point that what standardized tests often measure in younger children isn't so much their cognitive capacities as their ability to simply sit in the same place for a certain amount of time while taking a test.

If test scores are both narrowing the field of curricula for students who might be challenged to a greater extent than they presently are and are also causing some teachers to observe their students as having more limited abilities than they actually have, then it certainly might be the case that the existence of the tests are actually impeding any sort of spontaneous, natural learning. That is, they are causing learning to be even less chosen by the learner and are also causing it be even more predictable and predetermined by increasingly narrowing students' fields of inquiry.

Particularly in regard to the issue of students being given the latitude to initiate their own learning and feeling from its inception that they possess a certain degree of ownership of it, our current national testing program might indeed be doing a greater degree of damage than many of us can even imagine. For to send the message to impressionable young minds that the main point of learning is to prepare oneself to be tested on what other people expect one to acquire is about as far from Carl Rogers's self-initiated moth laboratory or from Henry Miller and his friends' spontaneous explorations based on their reading interests as one could possibly get.

Unfortunately, giving young people grades on a regular basis tends to be just as damaging. Although testing students at regular intervals can both rob them of a great deal of their initiative while, at the same time, predetermining what they will learn, grades and classroom tests leading toward grades present even more pervasive dangers.

Although testing young people on a regular basis can indeed cause classroom teachers to limit the curriculum of their students to subject matter on which they will be tested and to even pressure their students to learn it in ways that are unhealthy, quite often standardized test scores are something that many young people take far less seriously than the adults who are responsible for their learning.

While grades and tests leading toward grades are entities that tend to be taken much more seriously by students simply because they present a greater threat due to the sort of immediate disapproval that can come from parents and other adults in their lives. Consequently, they can send young people an even more powerful, negative message concerning their capacities as learners, even as human beings, simply because they occur much more regularly in their lives than does most standardized testing. In addition, of course, the power of grades comes largely from the fact that they are given to young people by someone they know personally (i.e., their classroom teacher) while test scores come from some vague, anonymous source (i.e., a testing service) with whom the students have no personal contact.

What often occurs in our schools, particularly within the whole results-driven culture in which we now find ourselves, is that standardized test scores and grades, because they both so often tend to reflect neither the process by which students gain knowledge and skills nor their expanded acquaintance with learning areas beyond the narrowly defined subject matter that is part of these evaluations, create an inherently dangerous narrowing of both teaching and learning.

This occurs when neither the process by which students learn nor the advanced knowledge which they may have acquired are given their proper due by educators simply because it becomes much easier to focus exclusively on objective measures such as test scores and grades. As a result, the sort of creative approaches to learning, which might be adopted when educators begin to focus more on the actual learning process itself and on the advanced subject areas toward which learning by young people might eventually lead, often tend to be abandoned.

Particularly, this might occur in regard to subject matter that is not covered by the usual evaluative procedures simply because it exists in the world outside the schoolhouse door. For example, if the financial security of our school would have been dependent upon student scores on the ITBS, we might have been prone to spending time teaching our students the skills and knowledge on which they would be tested on the science part of the test rather than using a significant part of that time to take them to places such as the laboratory of a physics professor at DePaul University.

Likewise, rather than taking those of our students who had written short stories, poems, or essays to one of the local coffee houses once a week so that they could drink hot chocolate or coffee and read their written works to each other, we might have instead been inclined to spend that time period back at school where the students would have been more focused on learning grammar and parts of speech.

At the same time, if we had become overly cognizant of specifically what subject areas our students would be tested and had attempted to steer their learning accordingly, we wouldn't have had the time to introduce them to a number of the advanced subject matter which we in fact did. These included such activities as learning about the theories of different developmental and cognitive psychologists in relation to the students' own evolving personal and cognitive development, building a model of a certain part of the DNA molecule at both the molecular and atomic levels, or learning algebraic theory through the use of Venn diagrams.

These were all learning activities that we had previously discussed implementing with our students, even to the extent of taking their advice concerning what they were interested in studying. So, as a result, they were able to experience the activities as being self-chosen. Also, because these lessons were both different in nature from what most students their age were learning in school and because they were the sort of complex activities that one tends to associate with the adult world outside the schoolhouse door, the activities often felt to the students as if they were entirely open-ended and unanticipated. As a result, they tended to be much more interesting than what one usually finds amidst the usual fare of elementary and middle-school curricula.

Of course, the next question in the minds of many people might be how educators can allow learning for students in their formative years to remain both self-chosen and unpredictable while at the same time maintaining the ability to reasonably evaluate it. For, of course, there has to be some way to be certain that meaningful learning is in fact taking place. Particularly, this is the case for high-risk or inner-city children for reasons that are obvious.

What we eventually ended up doing at The Children's School was to sit down at the beginning of the year with each student to create a learning plan for which the student agreed to be responsible. The plan included unique subject areas that the student had expressed an interest in learning, small-group classes that the student wished to attend, the manner in which the student would approach the gaining of certain basic skills or knowledge which he would need to acquire in preparation for future schooling, or even certain behavioral objectives that the student agreed he needed to address. Also part of each plan were the learning activities for which each teacher had agreed to be responsible.

The plans were all kept in a plan book, and at the end of the school day, we sat down with the students individually and went over whether or not they had in fact done what they agreed to do. If a particular student hadn't, then a general consequence decided by all the students at the school during a weekly democratic meeting was applied. For instance, one of the consequences voted on was that if someone had not finished what was on her individual plan at the end of a particular school day, then that person couldn't go to recess the next morning until that work was finished.

The point of the individual plans was to attempt to remove all vague, abstract, external assessments of learning and, in their place, implement a certain reality of encounter between teacher and student and between a single student and the other students. This had to do with the idea that personal responsibility, more than anything, is a matter of simply doing what one says one is going to do according to standards that one has actually been given the latitude to create for oneself.

Certainly, other schools that are not so much concerned with the empirical results of student learning but with what actually transpires inside young people as they investigate their world have adopted their own unique approaches to keeping track of meaningful learning without attempting to needlessly steer its direction in unnatural ways. However, in considering these attempts, as well as the more traditional ways of evaluating academic learning that have already been criticized here, it seems that there is a certain factor that administrators, teachers, and parents might do well to keep in mind. This is the intrinsic, often mutually exclusive relationship that exists between evaluations and initiative.

Initiative obviously has a very direct effect on how well young people eventually develop certain capacities in different learning areas. If a student possesses a greater degree of initiative in exploring some aspect of his world or acquiring some skill or bit of knowledge, he is going to naturally be more effective in accomplishing these things than someone with less initiative. However, if at the same time, the student feels that his learning is being judged by how successfully he is able to absorb and then demonstrate his competence with a predetermined curriculum which exists almost entirely within his classroom setting, then it is quite possible that this is going to dampen this same initiative.

If Carl Rogers had suddenly been evaluated by an adult in regard to his self-initiated explorations of caterpillars and moths, one wonders if he would have maintained the same degree of curiosity and motivation. Or if Henry Miller and his friends' street corner discussions of what one of them had recently read had been part of preconceived classroom lessons, would those discussions have maintained a similar level of enthusiasm? In both cases, one imagines not.

Initiative that stems in young people from their natural curiosities has to be, by its very nature, devoid of a certain measure of external judgment from adults. Otherwise, it is inevitably pushed back upon itself, and a stifling of interest occurs. While at the same time, if students' acquaintance with a particular area is contained within a controlled setting, such as the classroom that it is never really able to leave, it can likewise be smothered by the physical and mental boundaries of the setting itself. So the question becomes: how is it possible to not impede student initiative and curiosity yet at the same time have some way of determining whether meaningful learning is in fact taking place?

One rather obvious answer might lie in finding a way to synthesize initiative with accountability. And that, it would seem, is only going to happen if contemporary schooling begins to break down many of its self-imposed boundaries between school and the adult world which exists outside it. For as long as student learning is continually pushed back inside the same physical space with access only to a single teacher who employs a certain predetermined curriculum, then eventually that learning reaches a place where there is nowhere else for it to go. Hence, a sort of institutional frustration increasingly builds in both students and teachers.

However, if students were actually held accountable for developing the initiative to extend their learning into the adult world that exists outside of school, a very different relationship between initiative, accountability, and evaluation might begin to transpire. This could be one in which students were increasingly held accountable for and evaluated concerning their efforts to connect their academic learning to real-world manifestations of it, of course with the assistance of the adults who are part of their lives.

In this manner, then, the initiative to extend learning progressions might begin to become fused with accountability for such learning. That is, students could be held accountable, just as they presently are for assignments in mathematics or language arts, for imagining ways to connect their learning with real-world demonstrations of it. Again, they are going to need a certain amount of direction from their teachers and parents in learning how to do this.

Yet, if their school is willing to assist them by opening up doors into different parts of the surrounding community of adult expertise, and if enough adult experts are willing to donate their time, something very important might be allowed to occur. Exactly how this might be done will be covered extensively in chapters which follow. Suffice it to say here that the important new factor in the lives of students might be the beginning of the separation in their minds of learning and schooling and hence a greater feeling that their learning actually belongs to them.

I remember one twelve-year-old boy who came to our school after spending the preceding years in traditional public school settings, and as intelligent and self-aware as he was, he never really understood that at our school his learning could actually belong to him. Even in developing personal projects for one of our regular project fairs, projects that he was permitted to decide the content of with very little interference from adults, he always felt as if he was still "in school." That is, he was there either to please the adults who were his teachers or else play the game, which he had obviously adopted in previous schools, of attempting to provoke or test us.

However, when I would drive him home after school, he would leave all his confrontational behavior behind and once again become open and friendly simply because he had now left what was for him the setting of just another school. Often after he stepped out of my car and I was again struck by the difference between his school persona and the one that existed after school was over, I thought what a difference we could have made in this young person's life if we had been able to just simply take him out into the surrounding community to learn. For his past experiences at other schools had unfortunately conditioned him to believe that his learning was something that didn't really belong to him as long as it existed in what he perceived to be just another purely academic setting.

There is a marvelous description of this failure to realize that one's learning is one's own in George Dennison's classic book *The Lives of Children*, the story of the First Street School in lower Manhattan in the 1960s, a school which enrolled twenty-three students, all of them from poor backgrounds.

Dennison discusses José, a thirteen-year-old boy whose difficulties in learning to read stem largely from his inability to realize, due to his previous experiences at other schools, that anything contained in books or mentioned in classrooms belonged by rights to him or even belonged to the world outside of school. Instead, he believed that they belonged to some vague bureaucratic structure of which he wasn't aware. Therefore, Dennison's attempts to teach José to become a better reader had, more than anything, to do with simply helping him realize that this process was something that belonged exclusively to him.

As long as the measures devised to evaluate students are entirely created in advance and administered by educational pedagogues, which most of them now are, it seems that young people are never really going to feel this sense of ownership of their learning. Rather, it will continue to feel to them, as it did to José, as something that originates within some amorphous part of the adult world with which they are not in contact. Consequently, the very same frustrations experienced by both students and teachers in our schools due to young people often having no real feeling of ownership over their learning will continue to grow. Hence, the very same problems will tend to occur over and over again.

Alan Bennett's recent award-winning play, *The History Boys*, about a group of boys getting ready to leave a British secondary school in the 1980s for whatever college they would be accepted into, effectively dug into the heart of this question. That is, does one learn in order to simply be successful at demonstrating the results of that learning to others in positions of authority, or does one learn primarily to acquire affection for the objects of one's learning?

The boys in the school are all facing the coming exams that will determine if they will be admitted to Oxford, Cambridge, or some lesser college. Their long-time, beloved teacher Hector, who is infatuated with the literature and history he teaches the boys for its own sake, is being replaced by Irwin, a younger man, whose purpose is to simply familiarize his students with whatever knowledge they can employ to attain the highest possible score on their entrance exams.

Making the point that literature and history when used for an ulterior purpose exclusive of one's love for literature and history is nothing except journalism, the play includes one marvelous scene in which one of the boys tells Irwin that Hector makes them want to learn poetry as a conspiracy against the world—in other words—learning it utterly as an expression of oneself with no ulterior motive for doing so whatsoever. In fact, one might say, learning it in order to properly express one's alienation and one's pain.

This point, it would seem, is central to the argument being made here that for academic learning to become more meaningful for young people so that the very same frustrations don't continue to build in our schools, educators must help their students to begin to disassociate it from the idea of schooling itself and from all its trappings.

Grades and standardized test scores have a deep, logical flaw existing within them which tends to make them absurd. This is the idea that one can best determine students' capacities in various subject areas by simply evaluating how well they have absorbed skills and knowledge from preconceived curricula that continually narrow their scope—this narrowing taking place primarily so that students can then be evaluated by those who have designed curricula for these same subject areas by employing the same narrow parameters.

However, if the skills and knowledge that young people need to acquire exist only within subject matter that is constantly narrowed to produce certain results, there is a significant danger present. This is that the curiosities of students will be inherently stifled by the restrictive nature of the subject matter which they learn. How this might occur, then, is the topic of the chapter which follows.

Chapter Three

Subject Matter and Curiosity

Certainly, if we are to reform education so that much of the current frustration on the part of both students and teachers might be eliminated, one of the things that needs to be examined more carefully is the relationship between curiosity and the learning process itself. How significantly should the curiosity of young people be allowed to determine the actual scope of subject matter? What should be done when a young person's innate curiosities come into conflict with a preconceived learning progression? And quite simply, how might different areas of learning be organized so that the curiosity of students is inevitably the major factor that propels them forward?

Anyone who has spent a significant amount of time with children knows how their curiosity is almost like a life force that moves steadily forward from one object of interest to another. In fact, one of the hardest things about working with children is often simply trying to keep their attention focused on something which one is trying to teach them while their curious nature causes them to focus on anything that comes near to them in which they might have an interest, even some interesting thought that has just crossed their mind.

Of course, it is so easy for a teacher to be caught in the seemingly endless attempts to refocus the mind of a young child on a subject matter which one is trying to teach him while the child wants to ask questions about not only anything related to the particular subject area but also about anything which comes directly into his visual field, that often many interesting questions are either ignored or not taken seriously.

I can think of one particularly bright, somewhat precocious eight-year-old boy at our school. Because it was so easy for him to become distracted by his own thoughts or by the specifics of a particular subject matter that related to what he was learning, in order to teach him anything I eventually had to force myself to ignore all his interesting questions. Before he came to my school, he had been previously diagnosed as having a form of attention deficit disorder. Yet I don't think that the label, in this particular case, accurately characterized what was occurring within him.

More than likely, what was transpiring was that because he possessed such a vivid imagination, his curious impulses remained much more meaningful to him than did either the content of the subject matter on which he was being asked to direct his attention or even the possibility of any type of negative responses from myself or the other teachers for not doing so.

Over time, as I worked with him individually on a daily basis, I began to learn how I could actually begin to fuse his curiosities with the area of learning which I was attempting to teach him. This was to simply allow him to discuss his spontaneous interests with me until they reached a dead spot in their flow and only then begin to steer his attention back toward whatever subject area we were accessing. What I was in fact doing was simply allowing him to follow the flow of his thoughts until they reached a point where his inner dialogue had exhausted itself before I attempted to engage his mind, which by then had become somewhat of an empty vessel.

Roger Schank, author of the book *Coloring outside the Lines*, writes of an interesting experiment which one can try with children in order to illustrate the potential of their creative minds. This is to place a pop bottle in front of a child who is sitting in a room with no other distractions and then after leaving the room for a few minutes, upon entering again, ask the child what he's thinking right at that moment. Then have him trace his thoughts all the way back to the pop bottle. In doing so, the child can discover just how creative the flow of his thoughts can become, provided they are allowed to wander.

This little experiment, as well as my experiences with my eight-year-old student, it would seem, approaches the essence of what needs to be considered by teachers who would attempt to link subject matter to the interests of their students. That is, how might one effectively weave the internal flow of young people's thoughts and curiosities into the subject matter which one is endeavoring to teach them? Or, to stand the question on its head, how might one create subject matter from those same curiosities?

Fusing subject matter and innate curiosity very much goes to the heart of what educators are going to have to deal with if we are to begin to eliminate at least some of the current frustration on the part of both students and teachers from our schools. Too often now in too many classrooms, the two are almost mutually exclusive entities. The flow of young people's natural curiosities moves, unacknowledged by their teachers, in one direction while teachers introduce subject matter to students in a manner that often doesn't tap into their real interests in relation to it.

Part of this tension is of course simply institutional. Teachers are increasingly under the gun to be certain that their students are assimilating predetermined curricula in a manner that will produce the best possible scores on standardized tests. Therefore, there is of course not as much time as there should be for questions asked by students which have little to do with preconceived learning progressions, and so both teacher and students are led away from these questions.

Therefore, the obviously delicate relationship between subject matter and curiosity needs to be examined more carefully. Yet, before one can do that, the nature of the relationship between subject matter and knowledge probably needs to be also thoroughly considered. That is, is subject matter concerning some area of human endeavor the same thing as knowledge about it, or are the two separate entities that tend to function differently? And how exactly is subject matter currently used in our schools in order to facilitate a greater acquaintance with a certain area of knowledge?

Subject matter as it is currently conceived in the curricula of most schools is essentially a narrowing process. That is, it tends to break down an area of knowledge into increasingly smaller pieces. Even in many of the alternative schools which currently exist, schools go about the business of relentlessly cutting up areas of knowledge into increasingly smaller pieces.

Numbers and money become intricately programmed mathematical instruction; fascinating events from the past are often separated into different chapters in uniform history texts; great literature is itself too many times broken down into units of study which tend to resemble the CliffsNotes in one's local bookstore; and even the miracle of life and the mysteries of the universe are more often than not turned into isolated facts, theories, and schematic diagrams inside books used to teach life sciences and astronomy.

Piaget himself, the father of modern cognitive theory, in a series of conversations toward the end of his life with a French journalist, spoke of how if intelligence is to develop in young people, it must be motivated by an affective power and that the impetus for learning anything lies in interest, or affective motivation. This statement might, upon first hearing, seem rather obvious. Yet, for those who would consider it a little more carefully, it gets to the heart of what is currently amiss in so many of our schools, which is our failure to fully realize that neither intelligence nor genuine learning can proceed optimally unless they have the affective power of curiosity and interest driving them forward.

Obviously, this doesn't mean that certain facts, skills, and information cannot be acquired without young people being intensely curious about them. That is not what is being considered here. Rather, what is being addressed is how the development of intelligence in students in their formative years might be fused with the acquisition of knowledge. Conditioning young minds so that they can effectively absorb preconceived curricula is not at all the same thing, simply because this process leaves out the flow of curiosity as an integral part of learning and intelligence.

On the other hand, if one looks at the evolution of both learning and intelligence in the child as essentially processes of assimilation and accommodation, as Piaget did, then the affective motivation of curiosity becomes extremely significant. That is, as the child or adolescent absorbs new information or knowledge into previous cognitive structures that he has acquired, he will obviously not move forward with as much concentration or facility as he otherwise might unless he is intensely curious about what he is learning.

A younger child who is working with Cuisenaire rods to learn basic operations in mathematics will lose a certain amount of his curiosity toward the subject if he must manipulate the rods according to preprogrammed lessons that have been presented to him in advance rather than be allowed to simply play with the rods in an open-ended fashion in order to solve interesting problems or answer interesting questions that have been presented to him.

Likewise, a somewhat older student who is learning about the force of gravity will very likely have his curiosity dampened if his lessons on the subject have to do primarily with learning facts, theories, and equations that define gravitation rather than being asked to explore on his own, with the proper amount of guidance from his teachers, how space itself works in relation to this elemental force.

Each of these examples deals with how subject matter can either stifle or engender curiosity. In both cases, the culprit for dampening the young person's curious nature is subject matter narrowing a particular field of knowledge rather than expanding it. In the case of the child working with Cuisenaire rods to learn basic math, manipulating the rods according to a series of steps that have been decided in advance means that his mind is essentially focused on following a progression that has already been given to him. If he is allowed to play with the rods in an unpredictable manner in order to solve interesting questions or problems, then he tends to grow more curious as he focuses increasingly on his own responses to the material in front of him.

As for the older student who is learning about gravitation, learning and memorizing facts given to him in advance concerning how this force works means that, once again, he is focused on how effectively he can follow a progression that someone else has given to him. If he is given many of these same facts and information and then asked to come up with his own theory of how space itself might work in relation to gravity, he tends to become more curious about how his own open-ended responses might lead toward a solution.

Subject matter that present an area of knowledge to a young mind by determining in advance the progression by which the student approaches this knowledge is different in nature from a subject matter that allows the student to approach the same knowledge by constructing his own path toward it, of course with a certain amount of assistance from those who teach him. And the essential difference, it would seem, is that the former tends to stifle curiosity while the latter serves to facilitate it.

Therefore, if one believes that curiosity does indeed have an effect on both motivation and concentration, it would appear that it makes a great deal of difference which of these two approaches to learning a particular subject area a teacher employs with his students. In addition, it makes a difference not only in how intensely a student is engaged by a particular subject area, it also makes a difference in how well the student is able to actually acquire whatever he is endeavoring to learn.

The essential difference between these two avenues to learning, the one which employs a preconceived, systematic method and the one which employs a more open-ended approach which allows for more creativity by the learner, is that the first approaches knowledge through a specific progression which defines that knowledge while the latter approaches that same knowledge purely and directly.

This means that in the case of the child who is learning to work with Cuisenaire rods through a predetermined series of steps, his knowledge of how to add or subtract is something that is coming to him from a place entirely outside him. That is, he is acquiring it according to the preconceived progression. On the other hand, in the case of the child who is permitted to experiment with the rods as a way of determining just how the processes of addition and subtraction actually work, that same knowledge is emanating entirely from a place inside him, the rods serving as a tool to facilitate this.

Likewise, the student who is learning what the force of gravity is and how it operates through a text which systematically addresses such things as the effect of our sun on the planets of our solar system, or even something more advanced such as how gravity affects processes at the subatomic level, is gathering his ideas of what gravity is from a place that exists outside him. However, the student who, after being given a certain amount of information and knowledge, is asked to come up with his own theory of how gravitation works in relation to space is creating an answer out of his own thoughts and curiosities.

Whether knowledge and skills are acquired by following a learning progression which exists outside of oneself or whether they are obtained primarily by employing one's own thoughts and interests obviously has a profound effect on young people's curious natures. That is, acquiring knowledge from a place outside oneself tends to stifle curiosity while acquiring it by employing a path that one has created for oneself tends to facilitate it.

Therefore, if one accepts this idea that curiosity itself has a decided effect not only on how engaged students become by what they are learning but also on how well they actually learn, it would certainly seem that a significant challenge of contemporary educators would be how to implement more open-ended approaches to different subject matter that stimulate the curiosities of students in relation to them rather than to continue to rely on predetermined learning progressions which are in place before the students begin their school year.

In other words, how might various subject matter be presented to students in a manner that allows them to feel that they are in control of how they approach them from one moment to the next so that their curiosities are consistently driving their learning forward? Pre-planned learning progressions and curricula, often leading toward potential success on standardized tests, will, once again, not accomplish this simply because they exist outside of the learner's inner life.

It may also be the case that young people's curiosities have become a casualty of this sort of standardized approach, which is being increasingly implemented in public education and even in many private schools, because of how young people's curious impulses tend to be continuously pushed back in upon themselves when they occur in closed systems.

If one can imagine, for a few moments, being a student in a typical elementary or middle-school classroom, full of curious thoughts concerning much that occurs outside the classroom door, one might then begin to develop a fairly accurate sense of the scope of the problem. That is, the young person finds himself in a setting in which he occupies the same classroom, at most the same two or three rooms, for six hours or more each day. His teachers have pretty much decided for him in advance how he will learn specific subject matter, which he does by spending nearly all his time inside these same rooms. In addition, the student's teachers or other people he doesn't know at all periodically test him on how well that learning is taking place.

Yet, whenever the student's teacher addresses some subject which genuinely piques his interest, he begins to form all sorts of pictures in his head having to do with particulars related to the subject. These often occur in the world outside of school, a world full of adult concerns that almost never fails to engage young people whenever they are fully exposed to it. For example, his teacher may be discussing a work of fiction his class has read that has to do with time travel, perhaps something such as Madeleine L'Engle's classic children's book *A Wrinkle in Time*. The young person may have also seen a movie on television recently that deals with time travel, such as the most recent version of H.G. Wells's *The Time Machine*.

While his teacher and classmates are discussing different aspects of the book, such as plot outline, character development, and general themes, all sorts of pictures come into the young person's head regarding the possibility of time travel. Would it ever be possible to journey into the future? Where does the present end and the future begin? If one could travel into the future, would it be possible to change what occurs in the present?

There are in fact actual answers to these questions, based on real science, which can likely be found in the office or laboratory of any physicist working in the general area. Or if the student doesn't live near a significantly populated area, there are the e-mail addresses of reputable physicists from all around the country. Yet, in most classrooms today, if the student was to pose these questions to his teacher while reading *A Wrinkle in Time* and ask if his class could communicate with someone who knew the answers, this might well be where the conversation would come to an end.

That is, there would be no structure for allowing the teacher to connect subject matter within her classroom to those who have the knowledge or expertise to amplify on different students' curiosities. So the actual content of student interests, which in this case would be questions related to different aspects of Madeleine L'Engle's book having to do with time travel, becomes trapped by the physical parameters in which that exploration takes place, which is, of course, the young person's classroom setting.

Likewise, another group of children is learning about mathematics and money. More specifically, they are learning how the base ten number system, which they use to borrow and carry between different numerical hierarchies, is the very same one on which our monetary system is based. In addition, they learn the history of how our system of currency evolved from this and how the currencies and bartering practices of earlier civilizations might have emanated from different numerical systems, such as the base five system used by the Mayans.

In response to this, one of the students in the class starts thinking about how she very seldom sees her mother make change at the store because she always uses her credit card. Or if she buys something more expensive, she writes a personal check. So the girl raises her hand and asks her teacher to explain to her how exactly a credit card works. Can you just use it whenever you want if you don't want to spend actual money? Or how much does it cost to get a credit card, and how can a person get one?

Her teacher begins explaining to her and her classmates how a credit card works, how you can get a credit card from most banks, how the student's mother has to pay later for the things which she buys with her card, and that there is a limit to how much she can purchase with her card until she pays what she already owes, and so forth. Yet, at the same time, the students begin to grow confused simply because it is very difficult for them to understand the relationship between money and credit when they don't comprehend how our banking system works.

That is, for young people whose cognitive structures are still forming, unless they can tangibly see how banks work, how they invest money and all the rest, there is no good way to fully grasp the concept of credit unless they are somehow put in contact with an actual banker or someone who deals with money management. So, once again, the curiosities of young people in relation to the scope of a particular subject matter become inherently limited by both the closed, predetermined nature of the subject matter itself and also by the physical environment in which the area of learning takes place.

How specifically students might be connected with the world of adult work will be addressed in detail in a chapter which follows concerning how classroom teachers might become conduits between their students and adult experts from whom they might learn. Suffice it to say here that there are in fact two very good ways to open up subject matter for students so that their curiosities can be addressed more effectively. One, as has been mentioned earlier, is to simply expand the scope of subject areas so that they become more open-ended and unpredictable. The other is to regularly connect students with the world of adult work that exists outside of schools.

Of course, one of the best ways to accomplish the former is by implementing the latter. A teacher who is attempting to expand the scope of a particular subject matter for her students may certainly be able to merge it with other subject areas and to bring more advanced material into her classroom which relates to the specific area of learning. Yet, it seems, that teacher will nearly always reach a point where the actual physical parameters of the classroom will impede the further expansion of the scope of the specific subject area.

For example, a number of students at our school learned how the Bill of Rights in our Constitution works when we expanded this subject area by allowing them to study and debate hypothetical cases, just as students in law school do, and to conduct their own mock trials. Yet, if we had done only this and not actually consistently taken them to visit courtrooms in which both criminal trials and civil suits were being conducted, there might well have been a number of unaddressed curiosities still present.

These would have been questions about how a judge actually goes about running a courtroom so that the rights of the defendant are effectively protected. How are sentences actually handed down? Can the jury ask questions whenever they wish during the course of a trial? Can the accused speak in the middle of his trial? How are witnesses actually questioned by each side?

These questions obviously concern aspects of the law that no amount of classroom instruction, no matter how well-prepared or creative it might be, is going to be able to effectively address. And the reason why is quite simply that all of these concerns can only be fully addressed if young people, because their cognitive development is still evolving and because learning born of strong impressions is a significant part of how they apprehend the world, can actually experience a physical manifestation of them.

For example, presenting lessons to our students about how the rights of the accused, which emanate from the Bill of Rights, are actually guaranteed during the course of a trial might well have made this concept understandable to them. Yet, there still would have been something significant missing from their understanding, something which would have piqued their curiosities—to see how the process actually works when conflicts and tensions arise between one of the lawyers in a trial and the judge or between the lawyer who is representing the defendant and the one who is prosecuting him.

In addition, actually seeing someone sentenced for a serious crime, which several of our older students did one day when they witnessed a young man receive a lengthy prison term after hearing impact statements from his two victims, leant what they had learned about the law and our Constitution a gravity and significance that almost certainly couldn't have been achieved in any other manner.

Likewise, three twelve-year-old boys learned, along with me, quite a bit of advanced theoretical physics and even quantum theory. We learned Einstein's theory of special relativity, in which the speed of light is the one constant in the universe. We learned about his great theory of general relativity, which addresses the force of gravity in relation to the workings of both time and space. And we learned things such as Heisenberg's uncertainty principle, the particulars of Niels Bohr's quantum atom, and even delved somewhat into the concepts of real and imaginary time.

Needless to say, these were all significant expansions of subject matter for students this age who are learning physical science; although, all of the boys were extraordinarily bright, and our lessons together certainly aroused their curiosities concerning theoretical physics. Yet, just as taking our older students to trials clarified both their own curiosities and their understanding of our legal system, taking my three physics students to McCormick Place on the Chicago Lakefront to hear a lecture by Stephen Hawking on imaginary time, which I did, may well have put their growing understanding of the physical universe into much sharper focus.

For one thing, seeing someone who is so utterly disabled, as Mr. Hawking is by ALS, discuss such complex ideas with such clarity humanized physical science and those who study it in a manner which I don't think could have been achieved in any other manner. In other words, the subject, far from being only mathematical formulas and complicated theories, can have an incredibly human element. Secondly, being exposed to the remarkable drawings and schematics which appeared on a screen at the back of the stage while Hawking was speaking brought the four of us more directly in touch with the idea that studying the physical universe, in a very real way, can be just as much an art form as it is a mechanistic science.

One of the best ways to expand subject matter for young people, it would seem, is to simply connect them with experts from the world of adult work and academia who don't act as pedagogues in relation to a particular area of interest. That is essentially because the main concern of experts acquainting themselves with a specific area is not how they can impart its particulars to others in a manner which increasingly narrows it.

Their main concern is how they can employ those particulars to further explore the entire area and then to work with that knowledge for some utilitarian purpose. Therefore, the actual expert will often be in a better position to pique the interests of young learners than someone who does not possess a similar level of expertise and whose main concern with a subject area is to merely teach it to someone else by simplifying it.

For instance, a certain middle-school teacher is teaching his students the biological sciences by teaching them things such as how the process of heredity works, what the DNA molecule is and how it replicates itself, or what the different parts of the cell are. In the process of learning these things, the students learn them by essentially defining and then memorizing them. And, of course, there is a certain value to this.

However, if the teacher were able to actually take her students to the laboratory of a working biologist, who has agreed to spend a certain amount of time with them, the students would almost certainly become immediately aware that the biologist is working in a world wholly different from drawings they might have made of the DNA molecule or inheritance charts which they have devised.

That is, he may be working with different gene maps associated with the sort of genetic fingerprinting which is currently being used to determine the innocence or guilt of criminals accused of particular crimes. Or he may be studying different cells which might ultimately be used for prenatal screening of certain potential diseases. Or he may be researching how different viruses can be used to insert different types of genes into patients who need them.

In other words, the students who visit him would be put immediately in touch with the utilitarian function of his particular expertise. Consequently, their curiosities concerning the study of biology would almost certainly be piqued in a way that they couldn't possibly be if they simply stayed in their classroom to learn life sciences—the reason for this being that the young people can now see for themselves just how what they have been studying can be used in the real world. So this then, a consideration of what experts might have to offer young people that classroom teachers really can't, will be extensively addressed later in this work.

However, before that is discussed, it seems important to actually consider what sort of learning environment is possible that neither kills curiosity nor stifles initiative in the students who are a part of it.

Chapter Four

The Proper Environment

Exactly what environment will allow young people to explore different subject areas in the sort of self-chosen, unpredictable manner alluded to earlier in this work but will, at the same time, engender the sort of skills and knowledge which they will need in order to be successful in the world they inherit? More than anything, this appears to be a question of engendering the proper relationship between students and the knowledge and skills they are attempting to assimilate, one that will facilitate both their initiative and curiosity.

Obviously, this particular question has been around for about as long as educators have been asking questions about the purposes of schools and learning. Unfortunately, however, it seems that too often the question is asked within the confines of a particular closed view of what education entails—one that stresses that for learning environments to be effective, the subject matter with which students are acquainted must, almost by definition, be predetermined. That is, it must be structured in advance of students learning it.

However, at the same time, that is not how knowledge, skills, and one's increasing acquaintance with them tend to operate in relation to one another if allowed to naturally do so. In particular, if one looks at how any scientist, artist, businessman, or other professional who is thinking creatively looks upon the area of his or her expertise, it soon becomes apparent that that person is operating without any preconceptions in regard to what he is studying. Rather, he is following the specific area under consideration in an entirely open-ended manner.

When James Watson and Francis Crick uncovered the structure of the DNA molecule, it became essential to throw out the attempts of others who invariably looked upon the backbone of the molecule as always being on the inside and the chemical bases hanging from it on the outside. When Niels Bohr, Werner Heisenberg, and others brought quantum mechanics into existence, they had to discard the obvious, essential idea of locality—that pieces of the universe can always be found at a specific location at a specific time. And of course, when Einstein discovered his relativity theory, he had to begin by reimagining what everyone had always accepted as being true about time—that occurrences in the universe are always simultaneous with one another.

In addition to the discoveries of famous scientists, the same is of course true of any working professional who is attempting to come to grips with whatever he is studying or observing on the way toward gaining greater professional expertise. The historian writing about a particular period of history, the journalist following the thread of a story in preparation for a piece in the local newspaper, the investment banker following an unpredictable economy and market, the lawyer preparing a legal case, or the medical researcher investigating the thread of some possible breakthrough—all of these are examples of those who have had to consistently discard any preconceptions and instead simply follow the path of what is directly in front of them.

Yet, when it comes to how learning environments for young people in our society tend to evolve, quite the opposite appears to be true. Even many of the open-ended, organic environments, which one finds in certain schools which attempt to employ what they insist is a more child-centered approach to learning, are highly preconceived while many of the so-called free schools, although certainly not adopting preconceived, highly structured approaches to learning, are usually not genuine academic environments.

Unfortunately, a major culprit in this, something which can have such a dramatic effect on the parameters by which any school must function, is the conditioning and values concerning schooling and learning which often enter the school via the parents and children who are a part of it. Particularly this tends to be true of schools which attempt to give their students more latitude with their learning and, consequently, more responsibility for the obvious reason that any preconceptions concerning schooling and learning which have been conditioned into either students or parents can more easily creep into those environments than they can into those which are more rigidly predetermined by the adults who are responsible for them.

Therefore, if students, teachers, and parents in a particular school all have a more limited idea of how creatively and openly various subject matter might evolve due to their own conditioned preconceptions concerning how schooling and learning should transpire, then the subject matter taught is going to inevitably be more limited in scope. That is, if certain subject matter are going to be allowed to not only be expanded as fully as they might but also possibly even move into the world outside the schoolhouse door, then there can be no hidden agendas in relation to it.

Whether it's the need by school boards and administrators to enter into curriculum development so that test scores produced by students in a particular school district will lead toward greater funding; preconceived images by teachers of what their role should be, which often affect how they approach both subject matter and their students in a less open-ended manner than they otherwise might; or parental pressure on administrators for the inclusion of certain social values in the curriculums of their children, which filters down to individual teachers and then tends to limit how open-ended lessons can be — all of these can affect how subject matter might be limited in adverse ways.

Therefore, one of the primary, if indeed not most important, factors which needs to be present if subject matter are to be treated as expansively as possible is to keep learning situations as pure as possible so that a true continuum of experience can occur for those students who are a part of them.

Continuum of experience means that students are allowed to take their experience in relation to what they are learning to a point of completion. That is to say, natural curiosities, unique learning paths which have evolved spontaneously, or the inclusion of one subject matter into another, whenever that might be possible, are not impeded by preconceived adult agendas or predetermined classroom structures.

That is, if a student is learning a certain subject area, then that area is not needlessly narrowed in opposition to the students' own curiosities in order to engender certain external results in the manner alluded to earlier in this work. Nor does the teacher attempt to put himself in a position of unnatural authority in relation to the student, one in which he willfully steers learning progressions in directions which the learner himself has no say in determining. Nor does he make second-hand judgments concerning how well a student is assimilating a particular subject matter, assessment that might unnaturally limit the scope of what the student is apprehending.

On the other hand, what the teacher should do if he wishes to structure a learning situation so that a certain area of learning might be treated as expansively as possible is to attempt to determine the student's best possible relation to it and then proceed from there in the most honest, direct manner possible.

For example, a student is learning a particular area of science. Before the lessons even begin, his teacher should attempt to ascertain which specific interests of his might fully connect him to the subject area so that the teacher can employ these as a starting point for proceeding into it. If the subject is astronomy and the young person is more interested in the birth and death of stars than he is in learning to identify different planets and constellations, then that is precisely where his lessons in astronomy really need to begin.

For the best opportunity which the student has for effectively finding his way into the subject of astronomy is simply beginning with his interest in how stars come into existence and then burn themselves out. Then proceed by following this particular aspect of astronomy that genuinely intrigues him until it begins to naturally open up the rest of the subject area more fully.

For instance, learning about the birth and death of stars means that the student will soon learn of a star's inevitable battle with the force of gravity which means that he will soon learn how gravitation itself operates. Understanding this will then soon lead him toward an understanding of how the fabric of space itself can be warped by large bodies such as the sun. Soon after that, he will almost certainly encounter what black holes in space are, and then because these fascinating, mysterious phenomena themselves reflect the Big Bang theory of how the universe might have been born, he will soon become acquainted with that.

Therefore, an original, unique interest in a specific area of astronomy has led the young person toward all sorts of interesting and important considerations simply because these are directly related to that which originally piqued his curiosities. In fact, this is exactly what allowing young people to come into contact with a certain subject area simply by beginning with their unique interests in relation to it tends to do. It expands the entire subject for them in a way which simply couldn't have been done if their teachers had instead employed an approach which began by ignoring those same interests.

In the above case, if the student's teacher had proceeded with a preconceived curriculum which stressed, at its inception, identifying different planets within our solar system and different stars and galaxies and then proceeded toward other considerations, such as the birth of stars or the force of gravity, which do not necessarily have an obvious, organic relationship to where the learning sequence began, the subject of astronomy probably would not have opened itself up so completely for this particular student. The reason for this would be simply that he would then be following a predetermined learning progression which doesn't permit him to perceive as clearly the organic relationships that exist between different aspects of astronomy.

As a result, the student wouldn't be in a position to perceive the subject as an organic whole and to relate to it in that manner. Instead, it almost certainly would be reduced to a series of isolated facts and information which, although he might learn them sequentially, doesn't give him the same opportunity to directly connect them to each other and, in so doing, develop a clearer, more expansive, and, hence potentially more creative approach to the entire subject area.

Therefore, it would appear that one of the first principles of how to effectively structure lessons and learning environments so that various subject matter can be imagined expansively and creatively and so that the greatest degree of interest and initiative can be facilitated, is to simply allow young people's learning to proceed as naturally and organically as possible. On the contrary, it seems clear that what one should not do is to push areas of learning along preconceived sequences which don't allow students to be involved in the direction which they take. Otherwise, the curiosity and initiative of the students in relation to what they are learning will almost certainly be stifled.

In addition, if allowed to work out organic sequences for lessons with their teacher, they will tend to develop not only a very different relationship to what they are learning but will also tend to develop a very different relationship with their teacher, one that is much more pragmatic. That is, instead of viewing her as someone to whom they must necessarily sublimate potentially more interesting, unique approaches to a particular subject area in order to receive her approval, they will see her more as a guide who can assist them in how they might best connect their natural interests and curiosities to whatever they are learning.

In addition, the question of how to structure not just lessons in specific subject matter but also how to structure a learning environment as a whole almost certainly is a matter of adhering to many of these same principles of organic structuring; attempting to create the environment itself, piece by piece so to speak, from the individual needs and interests of the students in it in relation to what they are learning; and structuring it in a manner that proceeds only from those specific needs and interests.

This is admittedly not an easy thing to accomplish. For in developing not only a daily schedule but also certain democratic rules between teachers and students and in attempting to factor in the inevitable equilibrium of rights and responsibilities which are part of any learning situation or environment, one has to be ever cognizant of those forces and factors within a particular environment which, if not held firmly in check, will tend to impede young people's curiosities and interests in relation to what they are learning.

Often, in attempting to structure the environment of our school at the beginning of the school year in the most natural manner possible, we ran into all sorts of personal dynamics and outside influences which caused our endeavor to be more than a little difficult. For example, in sitting down with individual students to develop the most workable learning plans, desires of their parents which ran contrary to the students' own desires often became an issue.

When this occurred, as it often did, the issue of how to create a certain student's curriculum and structure his daily schedule when the wishes of parents not only entered the discussion but also occasionally won out over the wishes of the individual student, obviously became one with which it was often very difficult to deal.

For instance, if a particular student had no real interest in learning a particular subject matter that his parents were insistent that he become acquainted with and, if in the course of negotiations with both parties, we were not able to keep the particular area of learning from becoming part of the student's individual plan, then a couple of different negative consequences nearly always transpired. One, of course, was that it became very difficult, if not outright impossible, to involve the student in the creation of a workable learning progression when he had no real interest in the subject matter in the first place. Consequently, learning progressions would often tend to become predetermined by a teacher who was now working with a marginally involved student.

Another factor which would often influence how both individual and group lessons, and also how our learning environment as a whole, were structured were the specific competencies and knowledge regarding certain subject matter that our students would need to be prepared in before they left us for the next school which they would attend—particularly our older students who would soon be attending the local high school.

So, even though some or our students had little or no interest in learning certain areas of science or mathematics and would be able, we were certain, to acquire them in the future when a more immediate need to do so arose, we would on numerous occasions insert them into the students' individual learning plans in the least painful manner possible. As a result, just as when we had allowed certain parental agendas and concerns to find their way into these plans, a more forced structuring of the students' lessons and school days would occur, one that tended to put both students and teachers in the position of following through on approaches about which neither was necessarily enthusiastic.

These two extraneous factors, which on occasion unnaturally affected the attempt to organically structure learning at our school, are mentioned here for a reason—both are excellent examples of the sort of outside influences which can cause learning situations in many contemporary classrooms to evolve in the forced manner which can so easily stifle curiosity and impede initiative.

Yet, at times, it is nearly impossible to keep these entirely out of specific learning situations or the learning environment itself given that all schools are necessarily related to the society of which they are a part. In addition, of course, the rights of parents and the specific philosophies of schools and learning environments which young people enter are factors that will always require a certain measure of respect simply because of how they directly affect students' future learning.

Yet, all the same, in attempting to structure lessons and learning environments, the principle of continuum of experience needs always to be taken into consideration. For all organic structuring of educational settings for students in their formative years necessarily presupposes the existence of this important dynamic, one which is integral to not allowing the flow of a student's experience and curiosities to be impeded in an unhealthy manner.

If the manner in which a particular learning environment is structured does not emanate directly from the needs and interests of the students in it but is instead constructed before students even enter the classroom at the beginning of the school year, then those students are almost certainly going to experience both their lives and learning as blocked by the very environment in which they are being asked to learn. As a consequence, much of the inevitable frustration that occurs whenever students feel that there are impenetrable barriers separating them from where they want to take their curiosities, natural interests, or personal concerns in relation to their learning will almost certainly transpire.

Many of the frustrations that are presently occurring in our schools emanate largely from this one harmful dynamic—that so many of our classrooms are structured to impede rather than release the flow of students' personal experience in relation to what they are learning. So this then is the subject of the chapter which follows—a brief analysis of how educators might prevent this sort of blocked experience from occurring and also an examination of what the flow of healthy, unblocked experience in relation to academic learning actually entails.

Chapter Five

The Flow of Experience

One of the most significant difficulties with many learning environments is that they simply don't allow young people to finish becoming involved with that in which they have grown interested—to take either their curiosities or spontaneous interests to a point of completion. That is, often students will become involved with a particular area of learning which suddenly attracts them, and they aren't given the necessary amount of time to complete their involvement with it.

To fully comprehend this idea, one really has to investigate the notion that personal experience, particularly the experiences of young people, always has a certain flow to it, one that if properly adhered to moves a learner ever-forward in his investigations of his world. In other words, someone's curiosities and interests, unless they are unnaturally impeded, will always tend to move forward toward a point of completion and resolution.

This might be admittedly not an easy concept to understand, particularly if one is attempting to comprehend it only cerebrally rather than through the use of one's intuition. However, as anyone who has ever been frustrated by not being allowed, for whatever reason, to pursue his curiosities to a point of understanding knows, one is intuitively and immediately aware of this whenever it is occurring. And although children are often unable to fully grasp when this is happening to them, much less comprehend the reasons why, they still know when it is occurring and, as a result, grow frustrated.

Again, much of avoiding this frustration is a matter of not allowing the structure of a particular learning environment to become the problem itself. And of course, the structure of many classrooms today leads toward young people's curiosities concerning particular areas of learning, and their incentive to become more fully involved with them, not being given the necessary amount of time to move forward to fruition or else being blocked altogether by other subject areas being introduced too quickly because of a rigid daily schedule.

In fact, this is almost certainly why the issue of classroom control has become such a difficult one for many teachers to resolve, particularly younger, less experienced ones who might be less willing to turn a blind eye to spontaneously developing curiosities of their students that could interfere with proscribed lessons than older, more experienced teachers. I know that this was something with which I myself often struggled not only as a young teacher facing his own classroom for the first time but also after I had taught for a number of years—this realization that one often had to repeatedly nudge students away from what genuinely intrigued them in order to keep them focused on a preconceived learning path for a particular subject area.

Eventually, I got tired of it to the point that I ended up starting my own school in Evanston for this very reason: so I could in effect "lose time" with students whenever it seemed important to do so, that is, to simply allow the natural flow of their experience to direct where both my and their attentions proceeded rather than having to always stick to predetermined structures and lessons that were impediments to this same flow.

Indeed, what a pleasure it was, even after my school had been in existence only for a short while, to realize that because there was no longer a rigidly preconceived curriculum to which I had to adhere nor highly specific empirical determinations of learning to be considered, I could in effect lose time with the students in my school in this manner. That is, by permitting their spontaneously evolving curiosities and interests to be given the attention they deserved whenever they arose.

As time went by and our little school grew, it became increasingly obvious to me that not only should this natural experiential flow be somehow allowed to become part of the structure of our learning environment, but also it should in fact be a determining factor in how that structure actually evolved. In other words, in sitting down with students individually to create lesson plans or in meeting with them collectively at one of our weekly democratic meetings at which a number of the rules by which our school would be run were both considered and voted on, we attempted to design approaches to learning which would permit students to adequately follow not only their interests and curiosities but also any personal concerns having to do with their learning.

Often this involved something such as actually writing into someone's individual learning plan time which they might spend away from academic work so that the student could pursue certain interests that might come up unexpectedly and to which he or she wished to devote a certain amount of attention. For instance, there was one boy whose time spent at the art table, pursuing self-created, unique art projects, was very important to him, and so we literally wrote a certain amount of time he might have available to him each day, entirely away from academic learning, directly into his plan.

This would appear to be an essential concern in developing a structure for any learning environment which is likely to engender the sort of positive effects on both the lives and learning of young people, which is a goal of nearly all teachers. That is, to the degree that it is possible, how does one create a structure that will allow, whenever possible, for any unexpected curiosities or interests to naturally evolve? Otherwise, the natural flow of children's personal experience and the prevailing classroom structure will be at odds with each other whenever the latter doesn't allow for the former.

Of course, an important factor in how to accomplish this is the different learning and teaching styles which both students and teachers bring to any situation. For if the two don't somehow complement each other, what will often occur is that the manner in which student

and teacher each approach a particular subject matter will block the
natural flow of experience for the other. For example, a teacher
whose particular teaching style is highly organized and preconceived, as is the case for someone who tends to break subject matter
into small packets of information and knowledge, and a student who
has a strong need to immediately pursue any curiosities which may
suddenly arise within him will tend to have difficulties meeting each
other halfway, so to speak.

That is, the teacher will often experience that the student's constant need to follow his spontaneous interests are interfering with the
highly organized structure of her lessons, which most likely evolve
on a fairly rigid timetable, and the student will experience that because the content of the lessons tends to be so narrowly conceived,
there isn't time for him to thoroughly follow any naturally evolving,
unexpected curiosities.

Therefore, the structure that will most likely work for both will be
one in which the teacher feels that she can organize her lessons effectively based on the focused, highly sequential manner which she
believes allows her to best impart specific subject matter to her students, yet at the same time, the student's need to ask spontaneous,
probing questions is somehow woven into that highly organized approach.

At first glance, this might seem like an insurmountable difficulty
simply because the two different teaching and learning styles each
provides the very point of conflict which necessarily impedes the
other. The narrowly defined approach to subject matter of the
teacher doesn't allow for the unexpected, unique questions of the
student, and the student's constant need to become further acquainted with that in which he has suddenly become interested tends
to interfere with the ordered, sequential approach of the teacher.

Yet, if one considers what the healthiest possible relationship to
the actual subject matter to which the two are endeavoring to connect might be, a certain solution becomes rather obvious. That is, allow the subject matter itself to determine the natural flow of both

teaching and learning rather than permitting only the teacher's approach to it to determine how learning progressions will evolve. As a result, the student's explorations of a particular area of learning can remain open-ended to the point where he can genuinely inquire into whatever piques his curiosities while his teacher is able to allow for this simply by fusing her highly structured approach with the nature of the subject area she is teaching.

This means that by focusing entirely on the subject area itself rather than on preconceived lesson plans, empirical validations of learning to which the student is periodically subjected, or rigid, time-based approaches, the needs of both the student and teacher will be able to genuinely intersect. In other words, there is indeed a way to address the student's inquisitive nature in regard to any area of learning with which he is becoming engaged, and that is by making that concern itself the actual subject area.

If, for example, a student is learning basic geometry, there is a genuine opportunity to fuse his curiosity concerning why he should learn about different angles and line segments (i.e., how he can eventually use what he is learning about these things in the world outside of school) with a teaching style which is similar to the highly sequential style alluded to above. This is to simply develop a way for him to explore geometry in a manner that intrinsically answers for him the question of why he should become engaged by it as he learns it.

This could be something along the lines of learning to bisect line segments or figuring out the size of the individual angles in any regular polygon in a manner that fuses his learning progression from its inception with an interest the student might have in the study of architecture. That way, the reasons why the student is learning geometry are inherent in the focus of his actual curriculum.

For instance, several of the students at our school who had been permitted to build different structures of modern architecture by using LEGO blocks were later more open to learning some of the specifics of geometry simply because we had originally piqued their interest with the pictures of unique buildings they had found in books and then attempted to duplicate with the LEGO blocks.

As for the highly sequential approach to learning which the teacher employs, she would most certainly still be able to present the facts and information of geometry in smaller teaching units than other instructors might. That is, as long as each of those units addresses the basic concern of this student and others who may have similar curiosities concerning why they should spend their time learning geometry. In fact, what might well occur is that the students' teacher may be able to anticipate questions which the students might ask concerning the reasons for learning geometry by actually presenting the answers to these in the form of well-defined teaching units.

Many of the solutions to the sort of tensions which different teaching and learning styles produce might be alleviated by simply employing the subject matter itself to synthesize these different approaches. As long as teachers are willing to approach a subject area in the sort of open-ended manner that allows for unexpected curiosities and concerns in relation to it to be immediately addressed, they will still be able to teach in a highly sequential manner that introduces it in smaller units.

On the other hand, students who need a great deal of personal space and latitude in order to absorb a particular subject area could be given that by their teacher if she were to expand the subject, even creatively combining it whenever possible with other subject areas, in a way that allows those students any number of different directions by which they might approach it. Those who need a more delineated approach, which takes place within narrower parameters, could be given that by presenting the subject area to them in much smaller packets of information and knowledge.

In other words, by looking at subject matter as something elastic that can either be stretched or compressed to meet the needs of individual students, the natural flow of those students' experiences is less likely to be impeded by various teaching styles that do not necessarily complement it. Yet, unfortunately, what far too often occurs is that teachers attempt to shape subject matter in accordance with their particular teaching style before first attempting to apprehend whether or not there is a way to approach it which fits the unique learning styles of those students for whom they are responsible.

However, by viewing subject matter as being something that is potentially malleable, which can be either widened to introduce a broad field of information and knowledge to those students whose particular curiosities tend to require this, or narrowed to include the same information and knowledge in much smaller packets for those students whose particular learning styles require this more structured approach, the flow of students' experience can be permitted to move continually forward by synthesizing the particular style of the teacher with the unique learning styles of her students.

That is, unexpected curiosities and unanticipated personal concerns can be included when both teaching and learning styles are matched appropriately to specific subject matter rather than being predetermined before either teacher or student comes to a particular learning area.

It is of course a natural impulse of many teachers to adapt various subject areas to a particular teaching style which they believe will allow them to more fully relate to their students. For many of them, this process of ferreting a workable style directly out of the specific subject matter with which they and their students are engaged rather than out of their own personal tendencies as teachers will be at times a difficult one indeed even though it is one certainly worth pursuing.

However, experts from the world of work, pursuing their particular profession, tend to be more focused on a specific area of expertise than on their own approach to it. That is why, if allowed to do so, they might become role models of sorts from whom teachers can learn how to develop effective approaches to teaching and learning directly from the subject matter with which they and their students are involved.

Chemists working in their labs, attempting to synthesize certain compounds, or medical researchers determining how to inhibit or strengthen parts of our genetic inheritance as a means of fighting disease are certainly more attentive to the specifics of chemistry or genetics than they are to their own specific research styles; although, of course, they are also certainly aware of the latter. Likewise, investment bankers, attorneys, or accountants are more mindful, on a daily basis, of various economic and societal relationships, specific case law, or how to prepare tax portfolios than they are of their specific personal strengths in relation to their chosen professions.

Therefore, with this in mind, it seems as if it might be worthwhile to consider the essential differences that exist between classroom teachers and experts from the world of adult work in terms of how both approach specific subject areas which they are either teaching to others or else focusing on in their professional life. For if the nature of various subject matters can be apprehended in a different light so that young people might come more fully into contact with them, then this is certainly something which is worth considering.

In fact, as will be addressed in the chapters which follow, the questions of how and why our schools might do well to more fully connect themselves to the world of adult expertise outside the school need to be both asked and attempted to be answered. Particularly, it seems, they need to be considered in light of our new information age in which young people can now acquire much of the information and knowledge that formerly they could only gain access to through the teacher-centered, self-contained classroom.

In short, the purposes of education are going to need to be seriously reexamined in light of this new world in which connection with other people, knowledge, and information is now both universal and immediate. Otherwise, the self-contained classroom itself may eventually be in serious jeopardy of becoming increasingly irrelevant. That is, unless local schools, administrators, and classroom teachers begin to realize the possibility that there is now a new function which they might serve, one that more fully reflects the recent changes that have occurred in our Internet age.

Unfortunately, today's local school is too often attempting to prepare its students for a world that no longer exists, one in which information and knowledge flowed vertically, from the top down, so to speak, from a handful of experts toward everyone else. Now, however, information and knowledge flow horizontally between an increasingly larger, worldwide community of participants. Therefore, it seems rather obvious that our schools need to make more of an effort to connect themselves to this larger community and to the world of adult expertise that exists just outside the schoolhouse door.

Chapter Six

Educators and Experts

Needless to say, classroom teachers and school administrators have a different relationship to information, knowledge, and skills than do experts operating in the world of adult work. The former are primarily concerned with how they can clearly transmit knowledge from different subject areas to young minds, while the latter are of course concerned with that knowledge for its own sake.

The middle-school U.S. history teacher tries to be certain that her students comprehend what the basic causes of the American Civil War were, while historians such as Doris Kearns Goodwin or Howard Zinn, researching the Civil War era from widely differing viewpoints, are both still endeavoring to find different, unique aspects of it to write about, areas which many readers might not have been formerly aware.

There are of course a number of inherent differences between the middle-school history teacher and the historian. The first, obviously, is that the historian has a greater level of knowledge concerning a specific historical period, in this case the Civil War, than the history teacher simply because the historian is able to focus all her attention on simply exploring it while the teacher has other responsibilities in relation to her students. Hence, the historian has the time, energy, and initiative to become more fully acquainted with the specifics of Civil War history.

In addition, the history teacher and the historian have obviously different utilitarian purposes for becoming acquainted with this period of American history. The teacher's main purpose, of course, is how to impart knowledge about the Civil War to her students, while the main purpose of the historian is to explore the period in greater detail or else to explore some aspect of it that other historians might have ignored so that she can write about it and in so doing, educate the public at large.

Another significant difference between the educator and the expert, one that is central to the thesis of this book, is simply that the former tends to approach the particular area of interest in a much more predictable manner than does the latter. That is, the history teacher almost always knows in advance where a subject area such as the Civil War is headed simply because she is operating according to a curriculum that has been conceived prior to the beginning of her lessons. However, the historian is researching the area in a much more unpredictable fashion, looking for parts of it that have not been dealt with by other writers of history so that she can attempt to build a thesis that is at least somewhat original.

Likewise, a biologist doing research in his laboratory on the different types of viruses that can be used to implant genes in those who might be suffering from a certain illness because they have inherited a specific genetic insufficiency is following an entirely unpredictable path toward what he hopes will emerge as the correct virus. However, the average middle-school biology teacher creates in advance a path for his students (i.e., their biology curriculum) that determines how they will learn about things such as viruses and genes. That is, in contrast to the unpredictability of the researcher's work, the path of the biology teacher is highly predictable.

Of course, meaningful learning needs to be consistent and sequential, not haphazard and chaotic. Lessons have to occur in a sequential manner in which different pieces of knowledge from a specific area of inquiry build upon each other in an orderly fashion. Otherwise, students won't be able to fully absorb whatever they are being asked to learn. However, that does not necessarily mean that learning a particular subject area can't also proceed in the sort of unpredictable manner, similar to that which the expert employs, that more fully arouses young people's interests and curiosities.

The trick, of course, is to fuse sequential learning with explorations which are inherently unpredictable. That is, how might young people be guided by their teachers in a manner which makes a particular subject area more comprehensible to them yet also allows for the sort of open-ended investigations which are available to the expert?

Howard Gardner, in a section of his book *The Unschooled Mind*, writes of the institution of the apprenticeship, which in the past has taken place in societies less complex than ours. The idea was that a young person actually went to work for an adult expert who practiced a certain trade or vocation and during the course of the apprenticeship, learned the requisite skills employed by the expert. In so doing, the apprentice not only was introduced to the world of adult work in regard to a specific vocation but also moved increasingly toward becoming a member of adult society.

In addition, Gardner elucidates how apprenticeships, because they have primarily to do with the expert instructing the apprentice in a very concrete manner regarding a craft, trade, or vocation, tend to facilitate healthy cognitive development in young people which moves inevitably from concrete experience to sensorimotor to the sort of symbolic thought which one often employs to acquire a new set of skills, that he can then employ in a practical context.

Obviously, it would be very difficult to place large numbers of elementary, middle-school, or even secondary students in the workplaces of adult experts who would allow them to serve some sort of apprenticeship. For one thing, just the sheer logistics of regularly transporting large numbers of young people to adult workplaces on a daily basis would be nearly impossible. For another, it is of course unreasonable to think that adult experts are going to hand over significant responsibilities coincidental with successful performance of their occupations to students who are still in their formative years.

However, there is something else that can be done. This is to create relationships between students and experts which, although much of the work done by students would still be done in their respective classrooms with the assistance of their teachers, resemble that of a true apprenticeship. That is, students could actually be involved with researching different aspects of a particular subject area devised during the course of regular meetings with an expert at his place of work and then, under the direction of their classroom teacher, carry out their research back at school. In addition, of course, they could keep in touch with the expert regarding their findings through e-mail or text-messaging whenever they weren't able to physically visit with him.

Of course, the vast majority of the time, the adult expert working in his particular field is going to use his own research rather than that of students in their formative years sending their investigations his way. Yet that doesn't necessarily mean that those explorations can't have significant meaning for the young people who engage in them. This would be especially true if they felt that the expert was taking their ideas seriously.

For example, a reporter who writes interesting, quirky human-interest stories for the local newspaper might meet regularly with students from a nearby elementary or middle school, demonstrating to them just how he goes about finding interesting stories to write, gathering the relevant details, and then putting those details together into a piece of journalism that will be attractive to his readers. Then, after the students have developed a fairly good idea of how the reporter goes about discovering and then piecing together a story, they might actually begin looking for similar human-interest stories during the course of their own lives.

With the help of the reporter, with whom they could communicate by e-mail or text-messaging on those occasions when they couldn't actually visit him at the newspaper office, they could begin researching and then writing a story which depicts events in their neighborhood which they send to the reporter when it is completed. The reporter could then read the story and make suggestions to the students about how they could improve it. After revising it, the students could then send the reporter their edited story which he could take and, after revising it himself, actually publish it in the paper using both his name and the name of the students' school as a dual by-line.

Employing much the same dynamic, physicists at one of the large particle accelerators, such as Fermilab in suburban Chicago, might, via the Web, send students at a particular middle school actual bubble chamber photographs representing high-speed collisions of various subatomic particles. Then the students and their classroom teacher, by communicating with the physicists about how to read what is occurring in the photographs, could then create their own space-time diagrams, which are basic schematic drawings depicting the actual collisions of various particles.

The students could then send the physicists some of the diagrams they have created, and the physicists could, after commenting on them, send the students their own assessments of what they think is actually occurring in the photographs taken in the bubble chamber. Needless to say, if the physicists were able to send the students the message that their ideas and diagrams were being taken seriously, this would be the sort of partnership between experts and students which could exponentially facilitate the interest, knowledge, and self-confidence of the students in regard to the physical sciences.

Students in their formative years are in a position to gain not only a much greater level of knowledge concerning specific subject matter by partnering with experts, but they also most likely would have both their initiative emboldened and their curiosities piqued. Initiative would be engendered when the students feel they are being given a genuine hand in working with someone who is exploring a similar learning area while working in the world of adult expertise. Their curiosities, of course, would be piqued when the details of a particular subject matter become suddenly much more specific and, hence, attractive—as they would be if the students could observe an expert from the world of adult work actually making use of them.

This is the kind of message to young people concerning the learning process itself that is nearly impossible for schools, working in isolation from the communities which surround them, to effectively engender—the message that both their initiative and their curiosities can actually proceed in a limitless fashion when their learning moves beyond the barriers of external judgment by adults, of subject matter that proceeds in a preconceived, closed manner, and of restrictive physical boundaries.

But, on the other hand, the world of adult work and expertise, by its very nature, possesses almost none of these limiting characteristics. Although his employer may certainly present various standards to be upheld during the course of a person's work day, there are almost never any limits on initiative when the adult expert is practicing his particular trade or when he is engaged in some type of research that serves a useful purpose. An expert working in nearly any field is also certainly going to follow any curiosities he may have in regard to either his professional duties or his research. And although much of the expert's work day may indeed take place inside his office or research laboratory, his duties are very seldom specifically defined by the physical space in which he pursues them.

However, unless these meetings between students and experts take place on a regular, rather than intermittent, basis, the message to students of how their learning might evolve in an open-ended manner when their curiosities are respected will be a difficult one to send. It will often be swallowed by the more rigid approach to learning which the students will find back at their school, one in which grades, tests, and other such evaluative measures tend to kill initiative and narrowly defined subject matter often stifle young people's curious impulses.

Of course, experts working in the adult workplace simply do not have a limitless amount of time to spend either visiting with students at their place of work or else communicating with them afterward. However, if classroom teachers were able to become conduits, regularly connecting classroom learning to experiences with professionals working in the surrounding community, then this more open-ended approach to learning might evolve into something that becomes genuinely meaningful for the young people involved.

The crux of this approach would be information and knowledge flowing in a seamless manner between student, teacher, and expert. That is, after initially spending time with a certain expert, learning different aspects of a specific subject area from him that genuinely intrigue them, the students could work with their classroom teacher to fully digest this complex knowledge to which they have been recently exposed.

Then, after formulating questions that can be best addressed by the expert, the students, again with the assistance of their teacher, could contact the expert via e-mail or text-messaging. Finally, after getting a response, the students could return to the expert's place of work in order to discuss further what they have recently learned. This same cycle of contact with a professional, followed by questions to him that engender his responses and followed by a repeat visit to the expert's place of work, could then be reconstructed for as long as the expert is willing to continue working with the students.

That is, the teacher, in her role as conduit, would be continually assisting students in how they can take information and knowledge they have acquired from an expert, shape it into a curriculum that evolves from their curiosities, and then return to the expert so that he can further assist them in exploring a particular subject matter. As a consequence of this process, the typically closed approach engendered when subject matter is continually narrowed in order to produce certain test results and when it is only taught within the same closed physical environment of the typical classroom, might start to be reversed.

Of course, a number of elements that exist outside the schoolhouse door, such as how to involve surrounding communities more fully in the lives of students or how students might be evaluated in a manner that fuses initiative with accountability, are also going to have to change, and these will be dealt with later in this chapter and the one which follows. Suffice it to say here that the entire process would need to begin with classroom teachers adopting this changed role and, in so doing, freeing both their students and themselves from the sort of restrictive approach to learning that presently causes so much frustration.

However, if classroom teachers are going to have the time and energy to take on this new role of conduit, certain nonessential parts of their current responsibilities are inevitably going to have to be jettisoned. Among these might be continuing to teach certain elements of traditional subject matter which students can simply download on the Internet whenever they need to use them. Now that young people have such immediate access to knowledge on the World Wide Web that previously they had to acquire either from their teacher or the local library, teachers really don't need to spend the same amount of time teaching them certain components of standard subject matter.

Examples of these might be such things as the location of different parts of the human body apart from their actual function, geographical locations of various countries and states, details concerning various important historical figures and events, different scientific facts such as how various elements are defined on the periodic table, or really anything which students can simply retrieve on the Web instead of having it personally taught to them.

Of course, another responsibility of the average classroom teacher that might be significantly diminished would be the amount of time that she spends either meticulously following a national testing curriculum which is part of the current No Child Left Behind program, or else preparing students for the tests themselves. So many local schools are so dependent upon positive results on these tests which will maintain or increase their funding that there is often little time for even a proper amount of play or recess, let alone time for more innovative approaches to subject matter. Again, this is something about which Jonathan Kozol has written passionately and clearly in his book which deals with the restoration of apartheid schooling in this country.

Spending time either teaching students subject matter that they can simply download any time they want or else preparing them for entirely results-driven evaluations of their learning when teachers could instead be spending that time engendering both initiative and curiosity by taking their students into the world outside of school on a regular basis seems to make little or no sense.

As far as learning skills and knowledge which are essential and also establishing significant standards of accountability, there are certainly ways that both of these can be enhanced in the course of connecting students with experts from the world of work. One, of course, is to simply fuse initiative with accountability by assigning students the task of taking the advanced, complex information and knowledge that they have recently acquired from an expert and, with the assistance of their teacher and the expert himself, creating unique learning progressions of their own.

In so doing, the proof of whether or not there is indeed meaningful learning taking place would now be entirely in the pudding. It would soon become apparent whether or not students and their teacher were actually developing approaches to a particular subject matter that allow them to genuinely learn from the expert with whom they are connecting.

That is, if the students weren't finding ways to demonstrably absorb and then use the advanced material they were gathering from the expert, the unsuccessful approach they were employing would quickly become apparent to both themselves and him. An obvious, natural consequence for this would of course be that the expert would be less willing in the future to give his time to the students if they weren't going to be able to develop significant ways to connect their learning to his expertise.

In fact, there would be the opportunity for a great practical lesson to be learned by the students which would help prepare them for their eventual entrance into the current information age and global marketplace in which there is now such a premium placed on creative thinking. This would be that if one is not developing the initiative to connect with those who might expand one's horizons concerning a certain area of interest, then an important opportunity to do so would soon be lost. Needless to say, this is where accountability and initiative might begin to fuse in a more realistic manner simply because they are both occurring in the world of the adult workforce rather than only in a classroom setting which is separate from that world.

There are, of course, any number of logistical concerns that would need to be addressed if young people are to be connected with experts from the world of work on a regular basis. An obvious one, of course, would be how to arrange for transportation of a certain number of public school students to and from the workplaces of academics, scientists, journalists, writers, artists, computer programmers, lawyers, bankers, or any other professional who might want to participate.

Another, of course, would be the amount of research that educators would have to do in ferreting out those in the workplace who might want to share their time and expertise. Although this issue will be dealt with in more detail in the chapter which follows, suffice it to say here that administrators working in a local school district might have included in their job description the task of compiling a list of professionals working in the community who are willing to be involved in this sort of horizontal approach to consistent educational partnering.

Obviously, someone is going to have to do the legwork in order to establish the kind of relationships that go well beyond the average field trip taken by students to someone's place of work. Yet, if some type of directory could be developed for local school districts with the phone numbers, e-mail addresses, and MySpace pages of experts from the adult workforce who are willing to contribute their time and energies, this would of course facilitate the entire approach exponentially.

In our new age of high-speed communication, we now have a number of tools needed to break down many of the barriers between school and community that have been around for about as long as any of us can remember. Yet, all the same, two rather large impediments might still stand in the way if allowed to do so. One, of course, is the willingness on the part of administrators and teachers to let go of a certain amount of authority and control over the education of young people in their charge so that significant relationships can be established with experts from various disciplines who are not professional educators. In their place, however, a new, important responsibility would be established—that of the conduit who facilitates these connections.

The other impediment to this new approach to learning is, of course, how the adult workforce tends to be so exclusive of, or even has no relationship whatsoever with, the education of young people who are being schooled in its midst. Much work would need to be done and many changes implemented if the workplace of the expert is to be more deeply connected to the local school. Probably more than anything, professionals would need to realize the opportunity they now have in our computer-driven age to educate those young people who will soon join their ranks. Yet for this to occur, certain changes in the restructuring of contemporary society are going to have to take place—even a different conception of childhood itself. So these then are the focus of the chapter which follows.

Chapter Seven

The Process of Deschooling

Ivan Illich has written of how the idea of childhood itself can be very much a political term. That is, formerly, in different parts of the world and even in many cultures today, there was no inherent segregation of young people from the world of adult work. Prior to the previous century, clothes and games created specifically for children apart from those worn and enjoyed by adults were largely unknown, as was the idea that those in their formative years should necessarily spend their days separated from those who were older than they in the public institution which we now call school.

Obviously, there are certain inherent differences between children and adults that should be acknowledged by institutions such as our criminal justice system or by popular art forms such as movies or television programs. However, the former appears lately to have become too inclusive of young people who commit serious crimes prior to their cognitive capacities or their personal development coming to full fruition, while the latter often seems to increasingly pander to a distorted view of young people which is highly disrespectful of both their true abilities and their level of maturity.

Still, all the same, it seems reasonable to suggest that young people are significantly excluded from the activities of the adult world more than they really need to be. Of course, as the world becomes technologically more complex, it would be unrealistic to think that a certain degree of exclusion is not inevitable, certainly when compared to less complicated, agrarian societies in which young people regularly tended the sheep or worked in their parents' store from a very young age.

Yet now with the ease and speed by which we can all communicate with one another by e-mail, cell phone, or text-messaging, all sorts of opportunities for including young people in the world of adult work, opportunities that have might have been previously denied them simply by the need to be consistently in the presence of an adult expert with whom they might work, appear to be suddenly and readily available.

This means, as has been alluded to in earlier chapters, that it now might be much easier for young people to become regular participants in the adult workforce even if their role is to a certain extent limited. Before that can happen, however, institutions of adult society are going to have to open themselves more fully so that this participation by the young might occur on a consistent basis. That is, the tools of the adult workforce, those by which experts pursue their chosen profession, would need to become more available to students of all ages. Particularly this would be true in the lives of those young people who are yet in elementary and middle schools, whose acquaintance with the process of learning is still very much evolving.

These tools might be found in the laboratory of the scientist, the studio of the artist, on the computer of the stock market analyst or of the computer programmer, inside the film studio or theatre company of the playwright and filmmaker, or within the newspaper room of the journalist, as well as many other places. They could be made available to students in exchange for their participation and assistance in the specific area of the adult workforce which contains them.

For example, a class of middle-school students and their teacher could assist a biologist who, as part of her research, has to look at what must seem to her at times like a nearly endless number of charts showing the sequencing of the four bases of the DNA molecule by performing for her some of the methodical work of recording the different sequences in exchange for using some of the equipment in her lab to study the life sciences. Of course, the biologist would need, at least at the beginning of this venture, to be certain that the recording done by the students and their teacher is indeed accurate. Yet, after she was sure of this, a true symbiotic, utilitarian relationship might be established.

Or a group of students could assist a filmmaker in constructing the set of his film, helping to put together costumes, running errands, or being involved with any number of the mundane details that are part of the filmmaking process in exchange for using some of his equipment to produce their own short film. Likewise, another group of students, again with the assistance of their teacher, could be involved in some of the time-consuming research of case law for a local attorney, even assisting him in contacting those who might need to give depositions, in exchange for his expertise and the use of his law books in preparing their own mock cases.

What is being proposed here has obviously nothing to do with exploiting children by forcing them to unfairly work for adults. Rather, what is being suggested is a simple bartering system in which young people contribute their energies in the workplace of an adult expert, and in return, the expert provides them with the use of the tools of his trade and occasionally his expertise so that they can learn in a more interesting, open-ended manner by being regularly connected with the world of adult work.

Hillary Clinton has often said that it takes a village to raise a child. Drawing on this particular sentiment, it might also be said that it takes a community to educate one. It doesn't seem to be too far of a stretch to say that those who have been successful as adults in the contemporary workforce would be acting intelligently, even to a certain extent in their own interests, if they became more involved in helping to educate those young people who will eventually take their place.

Once again, innate curiosity and initiative are traits which can be either stimulated or destroyed in young people as they learn, and if the bulk of their academic learning proceeds in self-contained class-rooms in which subject matter is continually subjected to the narrowing process which has been alluded to earlier, the latter is often likely to occur.

Of course, the 500-pound gorilla in the room in all this would be getting large segments of the adult world to accept this sort of inclusion of and delegation of responsibility to school-age students. For although their vision is quite possibly an incorrect one, the majority of adults probably assume that young people, particularly those attending elementary or middle school, simply cannot be included in the adult workforce in some of the ways which have just been described. Obviously, what they're most afraid of is the potential damage that might be done to their own enterprises as working professionals if they were to allow students in their formative years to actually share some of their responsibilities.

Yet, there are any number of qualities and abilities that young people have by which they might contribute to the institutions of adult professional life. For example, certain social service and welfare organizations could benefit from the fact that many young people know the particulars of certain neighborhoods about which they could provide significant information.

In fact, in some cases, their information would be more accurate than that gathered by different professionals who work in a particular community simply because it is not gathered under the watchful eye of the case worker or police officer. In exchange, those students might be given the sort of access to the workings of these social service organizations that would allow them to get a certain eye-opening glimpse of the underbelly of the community in which they live that they might otherwise never be afforded.

Likewise, because the impressions of their world and also the acuity of their physical senses tend to exist with such heightened clarity in young people compared to that of most adults, they might be able to provide invaluable information to painters, photographers, sculptures, or anyone working as a professional in the world of the visual arts. In return, those young people could be allowed the sort of access to the tools of those people's trades in a way that engenders their own creative, artistic impulses.

These are the very endeavors that could easily stimulate both the curiosity and initiative of young people in ways which were alluded to in earlier chapters. Giving students in their formative years this sort of access to both the tools and the work environments of professionals would indeed accomplish a couple of important goals. One is that it would send the message to them that their learning, rather than being something that needs to be exclusively connected with the school which they attend, extends far beyond those boundaries into the world outside it. Consequently, their curiosities in relation to academic learning might be piqued exponentially.

The other message which they might receive is that the driving force behind what they can do with what they learn is in fact their own initiative. When students can closely observe on a regular basis how the activities and the explorations of the expert, which tend to proceed ever forward in a relatively unconstrained fashion, are in fact closely related to their own academic learning, a powerful message is being sent about where their learning might actually take them.

At the same time, however, what would be necessary to facilitate this type of increased curiosity and initiative would be the capacity of teachers to weave what students have been exposed to in the office, studio, or laboratory of the expert into the activities of their classrooms. If there were not the sort of extensive follow-up teaching taking place that was mentioned in the previous chapter, then the motivation engendered in students by visiting, learning from, or even working with adult experts would have no genuine outlet toward which it might proceed. Hence, it would then tend to reach the same stale dead end that all too often academic learning reaches when it is constrained by the type of artificial boundaries which one finds in traditional schooling.

Therefore, synthesizing schooling and the world of adult work would need to be very much a symbiotic, mutually inclusive process.

In the same way in which adult experts might be willing to expand their places of work to include young people, classroom teachers would likewise need to open the activities of their classrooms in order to more fully connect with the adult workplace. This means that educators would need to not only eliminate a certain amount of subject matter for which there would be less time if students were to spend that time learning from adult experts, but it also means that they would need to give up a certain measure of control in regard to academic learning.

The role that teachers might serve as conduits between young people and professionals has already been discussed in the previous chapter. Yet that is only going to occur if educators are willing to fully embrace it, and it will almost certainly not happen if classroom teachers don't recognize the possibility that meaningful learning can occur just as much in the world of adult concerns outside the schoolhouse door as it does in the dynamics of their own relationship with their students.

This synthesis between classroom learning and the world of adult work would only come to fruition if educators do indeed fully embrace it. Of course, when teachers are asked to give up a certain measure of control over their students' learning, particularly when they can see the obvious greater attraction which the world of the adult expert often has for their students than their own classroom, there is bound to be a certain amount of professional jealousy.

However, when teachers began to realize the opportunity they have to not only engender greater curiosity and initiative in their students but also to significantly expand their own role by facilitating new, exciting connections with the adult world of more complex information and knowledge, this, it seems, would tend to alleviate much of the professional envy which might occur.

Therefore, this proposed ongoing connection between school and the adult marketplace would possess two complementary components, both of them equally important. One of course would be the willingness of professionals to allow small groups of young people into their workplace and to spend a significant amount of time with them on a regular basis. The other would be a certain amount of abdication of responsibilities by classroom teachers and other educators in areas such as curriculum development and testing and a concurrent acceptance of greater responsibility in areas such as research into the work currently being done in different areas by adult experts so that follow-up lessons could proceed with greater purpose and increased clarity.

This is exactly the process we tried to employ at our school whenever students became interested in certain subject matter that was more advanced than that which they would probably have been taught at more traditional schools. Because there was no established curriculum at our school prior to the beginning of the school year and also because we didn't give grades or didn't subject students to regular standardized testing, we were able to be as creative as we wished in developing different subject matter.

Therefore, when students wanted to learn advanced areas of physical science, biology, mathematics, literature, or the arts, we often researched what might be available to them in the adult world outside of school. Consequently, our source material, rather than being that which is traditionally part of standard curricula or texts, became the latest books written by adult authors about different subject matter, the latest discoveries in the scientific community, the most recent popular trends in the art world, or even different interesting books written by adult authors for other adults.

In fact, this was exactly how I was able to create the physical science "curriculum" for the three twelve-year-old boys who learned advance theoretical physics with me. I started by reading *The Tao of Physics* by Fritjof Capra, and I became interested in the space-time diagrams which he used to describe how the collisions of different subatomic particles are diagrammed by physicists. Because I wanted to know more about this subject and even more because I knew my three students would enjoy creating space-time diagrams of their own, I researched the subatomic world further by reading Stephen Hawking's classic, *A Brief History of Time*.

While reading it, I was soon introduced to Werner Heisenberg's uncertainty principle concerning the inability of scientists to accurately observe a particle's speed and velocity at the same time. I immediately recognized that this topic would be genuinely fascinating to my students. Indeed it was to one student in particular who, even after he left our school for high school and I would run into him at the local bookstore, was still reading advanced theoretical physics.

Likewise, while teaching the group of students who were studying the Bill of Rights in particular and the law in general, I researched actual case law at a local library, scoured the Chicago papers for accounts of arrests that might be turned into interesting cases, and even watched reruns of the series *Law and Order* on television in order to generate the sort of hypothetical cases in which my students would be interested. These things I did rather than simply use a textbook which dealt with the U.S. Constitution and the law.

Of course, the next step, which is being proposed here as a way of expanding educational opportunities for young people, would have been to arrange regular meetings with physicists working at Fermilab or the University of Chicago and with local attorneys in the area as a way of establishing the sort of partnerships with them which have been described above. The important point is, however, that if teachers would rely less on traditional texts and curricula and more on their own real-world investigations of subject matter which extend into the adult world outside of school, then the possibility of partnerships with adult experts could be furthered exponentially.

Obviously, this proposed partnership between schools and the world of adult work, if it is in fact ever going to take place, has to begin somewhere. Most likely it is going to have to be initiated by school superintendents whose schools exist in large urban areas where there would be no end of opportunities to connect with professionals working in different fields. They could get the proverbial ball rolling by approaching universities engaged in specific types of research, large accounting and law firms, banks, local newspapers, computer programmers who are writing programs for different businesses, or writers and artists living in the area who are generally well known.

Then, when enough of these experts had agreed to be involved, specific arrangements could be made by schools to include small groups of students at all levels (secondary, middle school, or elementary) in the program. It would of course be essential that the number of students who are part of a particular group which partners with a specific expert be kept small so that there is significant interaction between the students and the professional and so that the need for the sort of behavior management by teachers, which so often occurs in larger groups, does not become part of the situation.

A school district could begin by implementing a small number of programs in those areas that seem to have the best chance of engaging students of different ages so that there is initially a significant opportunity for success. Then, when those begin to work, the number of programs and also the variety of exposures to different professionals could be expanded.

At the same time that these programs are being initiated, classroom teachers, by working with the professionals whom their students are visiting, could be developing innovative curricula which would allow their students to synthesize as fully as possible the information, knowledge, or skills to which the expert has exposed them.

For example, after a group of students meets with a geneticist who is working on decoding certain aspects of the human genome by looking for significant patterns that occur within the interactions of the four chemical bases (adenine, cytosine, guanine, and thymine), the students' teacher could work with them to develop a curriculum in the life sciences that fuses the study of DNA with the use of set theory in basic algebra to look for the existence of certain patterns that might occur in someone's genetic makeup.

Or, after meeting with a reporter at the local newspaper, the teacher might develop a program for expository writing that employs the techniques for researching and reporting a story that the students have discussed with the journalist. Or a curriculum for learning mathematics might evolve from students developing and running their own simulated bank at their school with the assistance of the local banker with whom they have been connecting.

While these partnerships are being developed in larger urban areas, where it would be easier to find more experts with whom to partner, information could be gathered on a national level that might eventually lead toward some sort of national directory of professionals who would be willing to make themselves available by e-mail, text-messaging, or MySpace, particularly to students who live in rural areas, where there is not the same potential personal access to the world of professional expertise.

Of course, none of this proposed expansion of education into the world of adult work is ever going to happen without those who educate our young people first seeing that it is necessary, and that is not going to happen unless they first recognize how many of our present approaches to learning, particularly those which take place in most public schools, thoroughly stifle both curiosity and initiative. Then, if this indeed occurs, the sort of focused, organized effort to connect learning to the world of adult expertise so that both these qualities can be stimulated might actually be engendered.

There is also one more important issue. This is simply the idea that the knowledge, skills, and information which young people will need in order to be successful in the world they will eventually enter exist not primarily in the classroom but in that same world into which the students are headed. That is, specific abilities, such as writing well or working with numbers, can be defined primarily by how they will be used by students when they enter the adult workforce. This means, in effect, that those abilities are continually evolving as the society in which they are employed undergoes certain changes.

For example, in our computer-driven age, mathematical thinking, particularly that used in performing basic algebra, has now become significantly more important than it was fifteen or twenty years ago.

At the same time, information moves so fast, and everyone now wants to retrieve it so quickly, that certain other skills, such as being able to add long columns of figures or using paper and pencil to divide by a two- or three-digit divisor, are becoming rapidly outmoded as more and more people now simply resort to the use of handheld calculators or the one found on their computer.

Likewise, the average layperson now has significantly greater access to the worlds of both physical and life sciences due to what can be retrieved on the World Wide Web and due to recent books by experts such as Stephen Hawking and James Watson, books which have educated so many people about complex aspects of these two subject areas which were formerly out of their reach. Consequently, the average elementary, middle-school, or even secondary teacher may be no longer the best person to provide young people with information or knowledge about either the physical universe or our own biological world in the sort of exclusive manner that teachers traditionally have.

This doesn't mean, by any stretch of the imagination, that teachers no longer have the capacity to bring the sort of complex information and knowledge into their classrooms that will connect their students to similar complexities to be found in the world of adult work. It simply means that they might need to now focus increasingly on how to connect their students with those experts who are more versed in such knowledge. At the same time, our methods and systems of education have always suffered, it seems, from turning a blind eye to how the capacities that young people need to acquire to become successful can often best be found in the very milieu in which they will one day pursue that success—that is, in the adult workforce itself.

Finally, as will be dealt with in the chapter which follows, the partnering of schools with the workplaces of experts would present a genuine opportunity to address some of the inequities in our schools which seem to forever plague us. That is, students who attend certain inner-city schools which do not have the same amount of resources due to socioeconomics as schools that exist in wealthier suburban neighborhoods, might be given the same opportunities to connect with adult experts in all different areas if a program for a certain wide geographical area were established which gave everyone an equal opportunity to make these type of connections.

When all is said and done, opening the schoolhouse door more completely into the world outside might well be the best chance we have in this society to level the playing field of educational opportunity. Schools that exist in certain lower socioeconomic neighborhoods will always be significantly at the mercy of the lesser amount of monies that they have to educate their young—that is, unless that education begins to move into a world of adult experts to whom all would have direct access.

Whether it's students from the South Bronx in New York City connecting with physics professors at Columbia, or those in North Lawndale on Chicago's West Side having access to investment bankers in the nearby Loop, or those in Appalachia using the Internet to learn from writers and artists around the country, it seems that there might be a real opportunity here. That would be to initiate an education for young people from the outside in, so to speak, by attempting to reach them from different parts of the very society into which they are headed.

Chapter Eight

A New Opportunity

As was addressed in earlier chapters, an overly results-driven approach to educating students in their formative years, such as that which emanates from our current national testing program, tends to destroy initiative while the ever-increasing narrowing of subject matter which is found in many classrooms today tends to stifle curiosity. In addition, of course, the existence of these two destructive dynamics tends to be even more prevalent in inner-city schools, which are often heavily dependent upon the continued financing which can best be achieved through higher test scores.

Once again, Jonathan Kozol has written often and brilliantly about the damaging effects of the current No Child Left Behind program on inner-city youth. More specifically, he has addressed the stifling effects engendered by teaching narrowly defined, test-driven subject matter to students in lieu of other subject areas which might enrich their lives by broadening them. In some schools, things like art and music have even been eliminated altogether from the curriculum not because there isn't the funding for them but because they simply aren't areas of learning that will be tested.

In addition, in his book *Savage Inequalities*, Kozol addressed the inequities that appear between schools in East St. Louis, North Lawndale, and the South Bronx and those in communities such as Winnetka in suburban Chicago or the affluent community of Riverdale in New York City. As much as anything, Kozol focused in

this work on the basic inequities that exist between the actual classroom environments of schools in these different socioeconomic
neighborhoods. These concerned such things as the number of students in different classrooms, the physical upkeep of different facilities, degrees of access which students might have to books or computers, and even the quality of teaching which exists in different
classrooms.

Unfortunately, despite the passionate pleas of Kozol and others to
address the inequities that exist between the schools of the rich and
the poor in our society, little has in fact changed. The same inequities
continue to exist despite the speeches that are given during each new
cycle of presidential politics, and increasingly desperate solutions
seem to be tried.

Recently, there was a report on a morning news program detailing
how students in a certain inner-city school were actually being paid
to learn. As one noted educator said when asked his opinion of this
method, this approach is not only demeaning to young people because it suggests to them that they can't learn unless they are paid to
do so, but also when employed with minority groups of students, it
almost borders on being overtly racist.

At the same time, as insightful and passionate as Kozol's analyses
are, his proposed solutions and the solutions of many other educational reformers end with how schools in inner-city neighborhoods
might be made more comparable to those of their suburban counterparts rather than seeking ways for young people living in these
neighborhoods to actually learn outside of school itself, which is exactly what may be needed.

If inner-city schools are ever going to have the same access to educational resources, quality teachers, or even the same attractive
physical environments as those schools which exist in wealthier
neighborhoods, this means ultimately that somehow those in our society who are wealthier are going to have to be willing to in effect
take some of the money that is being spent to educate their own children and then see to it that young people who are being schooled in

what are presently referred to as "disadvantaged" neighborhoods receive a share of that same money. Needless to say, particularly because it concerns the one thing that tends to be most important to people, their children, it seems at best naïve to think that this is ever really going to occur on any type of consistent basis.

Unfortunately, there are in fact only a certain amount of educational resources to be distributed in any given society. That is, there is only so much money which can be spent on education, only so many quality teachers, only so many resources to be divided among different school districts, and only so much collective will to distribute these things equitably, so that the answer for some of the young people in our society whose lot may be to attend schools which are inferior to others in different socioeconomic neighborhoods might indeed be an approach to education which engages the larger community of which their schools are a part.

John Holt has written of how the purpose of schooling is often simply to produce the sort of learning that takes place only so more learning can take place, without an eventual outlet to employ that learning or to connect it with the world outside of school. For children who grow up in affluent neighborhoods, where it is often expected that they will go to college and enter the job market at a significantly high level, the purpose of school then obviously becomes one of simply attaining the sort of education that will allow them to enjoy the sort of affluent life that they see transpiring all around them. Therefore, they are often quite willing to engage in academic learning simply so that they can receive more academic learning.

However, in many inner-city neighborhoods, there is of course a very different dynamic present. There, young people are not able to see many adults who have given themselves a better life by engaging in learning for learning's sake, this being true for a couple of rather obvious reasons. One is simply that many people who grow up in a particular impoverished inner-city neighborhood and then go on to become visibly successful, economically and otherwise, tend to leave the neighborhood in order to live in a better one. This is of course both natural and inevitable, for it is simply human nature to want to live in a more physically attractive, less stressful world.

The other reason is that, unfortunately, in many inner-city neighborhoods, status often does not accrue only from becoming a respectable, self-sufficient member of society. But also, it often exists in the world of gangs, drugs, and prison-culture dress and speech. So when children who go to school in these neighborhoods are not able to regularly perceive the possible connection between the sort of learning for learning's sake which tends to exist in school and becoming successful in one's own community, there is less reason for them to engage in academic learning simply so they can have access to more learning. This particular dynamic is also quite obviously a matter of human nature.

Unfortunately, a large part of the difficulty of developing a more effective model for learning in inner-city neighborhoods is that that those who create many of the solutions have themselves spent so little time living or working in these neighborhoods on a consistent basis. Having spent seven years teaching in the inner-city neighborhood of Englewood on Chicago's South Side as the only white person in the school and then every afternoon driving back to my almost exclusively white neighborhood in the suburbs, I learned how important it is to spend a significant amount of time in a neighborhood which is different from one's own before one can see it clearly—that is, to begin to perceive it clearly by actually beginning to confront many of the prejudices and values in oneself by which one has been previously conditioned.

However, all the same, it shouldn't take a huge amount of imagination to consider just how a young person who attends school in a typical inner-city neighborhood might begin to look upon learning which only leads toward more learning, particularly when one perceives so little social or economic advantage for doing so, as being at times almost just plain silly. Certainly, despite all the slogans and platitudes hurled at him about the value of staying in school, he might often perceive such learning as being something that is done for no good reason.

Yet, if the academic learning of that same young person were to be consistently connected, in ways which have been discussed in earlier chapters, with adult experts from the city in which he lives, particularly with those from his own community, then it seems the possible reasons for engaging in such learning might begin to become clearer to him. For example, if he were part of a small group of students who visits regularly with a botanist at the local conservatory—studying, dissecting, and even drawing all types of plant life—then when classroom learning which addresses the subject of plants, botany, or the life sciences takes place, he will likely have more of a reason to let himself be engaged by it.

I know that when we took students from our school in Evanston to visit The Garfield Park Conservatory, one of the largest continuous greenhouses in the world on Chicago's Near West Side, particularly when we let them bring their sketchpads and sit for a significant period of time making drawings of different plants, the entire atmosphere of the place would tend to have its effect on some of the students. That is, just the multitude of different plants in many different greenhouses, added to the incredible oxygen-rich atmosphere of the place, sent a powerful message to our students about the magic properties of plant life, something which far transcended what could be learned in a guidebook or school text detailing different types of plants.

However, once again, what is being suggested here is not just field trips to such a place or even carefully planned programs for groups of schoolchildren. What is being proposed are actual continuous working relationships between experts—in this case, a botanist who either works for the conservatory or else uses it to engage in his research—and small groups of young people, so that, especially for inner-city students, the reasons for their learning exist just as much outside the classroom as they do within it.

Another example of how students from inner-city schools might be meaningfully connected with the world of adult expertise would be meeting regularly with an investment banker, accountant, or attorney who works in the financial center of the city, such as on LaSalle Street in downtown Chicago or in the financial district of Lower Manhattan in New York City—that is, somewhere that might seem to a group of impressionable young students from the West Side of Chicago or the South Bronx as if it were almost on another planet.

In doing so, the students, as part of their mathematics curriculum or in learning about the U.S. Constitution, might be able to see more clearly the reasons for engaging in both these subject areas as their academic learning is fused with adult endeavors toward which such learning inevitably leads. However, they would also learn this lesson in the context of a world which, because of not only its potential differences from the community in which they live but also because of the obvious power and influence this world might have when seen through their eyes, might significantly heighten the appeal of their own academic learning.

There is also a possible indirect benefit which might accrue from students who attend inner-city schools establishing relationships with professionals who are in positions of power. This would be a greater degree of concern which might germinate in the minds of the adult experts for the extraordinary difficulties which young people who must grow up in impoverished, violent neighborhoods often face. Just this past week in Chicago, there was another gang-related murder of a teenager just outside of one of the high schools on Chicago's Near West Side. Although it happened only a few days ago, mention of it has already significantly disappeared from the local papers. For unfortunately, out of sight in a heavily segregated city such as Chicago also often means out of mind.

However, if for instance, a small group of students who had established a significant partnering relationship with a successful investment banker or attorney working in downtown Chicago actually knew friends or family members of the murdered student, then this might well frame his story in a whole different light in the mind of the professional with whom the students were connecting. That is, it might not soon vanish from his mind as just another inner-city tragedy, but would instead exist in the world of young people whom he has gotten to know personally.

As a result, through the adult expert's possible connections and influences, certain programs and measures might be initiated that would make some sort of lasting difference in the particular neighborhood in which the violence took place. For instance, one possible solution, one which would obviously need to evolve over a certain length of time, might be the establishment of a center by the investment banker which educates students on how their families' monies might be intelligently invested so that a reasonably healthy financial portfolio might ensue. Or likewise, the establishment of a law center which trains young people and their families about their specific legal rights in regard to such issues as housing, crime, and schooling.

Unfortunately, too often when people in positions of power and influence get involved in trying to make a difference in inner-city neighborhoods, it is done through some large agency such as the United Way or by a wealthy individual setting up a fund which provides for something like inner-city youths' attending college. As noble as these enterprises might be, the motivation for their existence seldom arises from someone being personally affected by what goes on in certain neighborhoods—the reason for this being that the people who are contributing are usually not very familiar with young people who live there and are also not working on a consistent basis with those who might have first-hand knowledge of the difficulties and tragedies which occur in those same neighborhoods.

In addition, if young people who attend schools in certain marginalized neighborhoods could be connected with professionals working in their own community, this might have a different, perhaps even more powerful, effect. This would be especially true if the students' academic learning could be connected as fully as possible with the daily endeavors of these adult experts. For then the students could actually see within the context of their own community how certain adults are employing the same subject areas that they are learning in school to successfully make their way in the world.

In addition, if professionals who work in the inner city were to regularly connect with the schools there, the quality of those schools themselves might significantly improve. This might be true for the obvious reason that as students gained greater access to advanced information, knowledge, and skills as a result of partnerships initiated between them and experts from the community, then that same advanced knowledge might well trickle down, so to speak, to other students and teachers in the school. Hence a cycle of advanced knowledge and cutting-edge information might indeed flow between inner-city schools and the communities in which they exist that would markedly improve those schools.

In the final analysis, the great equalizer in our society which would give students attending schools that are not now of the same caliber as those in other neighborhoods a better chance to receive a quality education might be simply giving them an equal chance to be connected to the larger community of which all the different schools are a part.

Students in the South Bronx and those who live in Riverdale who are partnering with the same physicist at Columbia University would both be exposed to a similar level of expertise. Likewise, students from Chicago's South Side neighborhood of Englewood and those from the wealthy North Shore suburbs of Glencoe or Winnetka who are learning from the same laboratory technician working in one of the larger hospital complexes in the city are also both having their lives and learning enriched in the very same ways.

Finally, as was alluded to in the introductory chapter, so many inner-city schools often rely so desperately on achieving certain scores on standardized tests to keep their funding that it can become very easy for the existence of these tests themselves to become a well-disguised form of institutional racism aimed at keeping certain racial or socioeconomic groupings permanently disenfranchised.

That is, because of the inferior schooling which many inner-city students receive, because of the difficulties with which they have to contend in coming of age in certain neighborhoods, and even because a large number of children from certain minority groupings are being raised by a single mother, it is almost inevitable that the test scores of those students are not going to be as high as those who have all the advantages that these young people don't have.

Therefore, the whole process of evaluating learning through performance on standardized tests can become, intentionally or not, a well-oiled self-fulfilling prophecy which, when combined with the fact that educational opportunity is often based largely on one's scores on these tests, can keep certain groupings in our society permanently marginalized.

One possible way out of this cycle is to simply replace many of the test scores with the sort of demonstration of creative achievement that might be engendered when students partner with experts. For instance, it would seem that students creating and then implementing research projects of their own which germinate from their experience working with a certain professional might be a much better indication of the students' facilities in a certain area than the scores on a particular test which focus, in a much less complex, narrowly defined manner, on the same subject area.

Of course, acquiring basic skills, particularly for those students living and being educated in certain marginalized segments of society, are always going to be important. Yet, at the same time, it's hard to imagine how the skills of reading, writing, working with numbers, or developing critical or scientific thinking could be learned any better than when they emanate from students being involved with and developing something larger in the context of real-world activities.

Researchers working in their laboratories are often critically involved with mathematics and critical thought. Investors are involved with not only basic mathematics but also with the sort of algebraic thought, although they might not identify it as such, which allows them to identify various economic, market-driven patterns. Attorneys are of course very much involved with not only expressing their opinions clearly in writing but also with the sort of analytical thought by which they prepare their cases. Journalists are of course involved with how to write clear themes using concise sentences. And filmmakers and artists of all sorts are pursuing the ever-finer development of their aesthetic sense, often through the use of certain high-level conceptual thinking.

Obviously, creating these types of partnerships between young people, particularly younger students, and working professionals is going to take a significant amount of organization and will power. Yet, again, if school boards, administrators, and classroom teachers were willing to let go of certain aspects of their basic roles, such as the amount of time which they presently spend preparing students for success on high-stakes standardized tests, in lieu of taking on a new responsibility of serving as conduits between young people and adult expertise, then the collective will to accomplish this might indeed be summoned.

Once again, the knowledge, skills, and expertise that students need to acquire in order to be successful in the world they will inherit exist in that very world itself and not so much, as was previously imagined, in self-contained classrooms which attempt to teach that knowledge and those skills in isolation from the surrounding community. With this in mind, what might really be necessary in order to more fully connect young people with the capabilities they will need for their future success in our ever-expanding global marketplace is the collective will of schools that are willing to adopt a changed role in our society, and working professionals who are willing to take on a new role of being educators for the young people in their midst.

Chapter Nine

Homeschooling and Online Learning

As many of our schools, particularly our public schools, are called more and more into question, increasing numbers of parents are deciding to homeschool their children and/or, with the advent of the World Wide Web, resorting to online learning programs to educate them. Of course, the homeschooling movement has been prevalent in our society since the early 1970s, fueled in large measure by the critiques of public schooling that existed in the writings of authors such as John Holt, whose classic books *How Children Learn* and *How Children Fail* were a significant impetus that initiated the increased desire by many parents to remove their children from traditional schooling.

There are of course many disparate reasons why parents make the decision to teach their children at home. One, of course, is that they are simply dissatisfied with the local public schools and believe that they can do a better job of teaching their offspring. Another reason, which has been well documented for a number of years now in stories in magazines or newspapers, is that parents decide to homeschool their children so that they can give them the sort of religious education that they feel they would be denied in either the public or private schools to which they might have access.

There are, of course, cases of parents who are overprotective and consequently are unable to let go of their children enough to let them attend school by relinquishing a certain measure of control of their upbringing and learning. These parents are almost certainly in the minority of homeschooling parents, although they do exist. This is something to which I can attest because I saw some parents who came to my school who had formerly been homeschooling parents for this exact reason: they just couldn't bring themselves to put their children in the hands of somebody they didn't know for the greater part of a day.

There are many more reasons than just these for the homeschooling option, and they of course stem from a myriad of different concerns. In fact, the spectrum of reasons why parents choose to homeschool their children is about as broad as the American landscape itself.

Some of these are: people adhering to very strict, conservative religious principles; free-spirited hippies from the baby boom generation or else the children of baby boomers who have adopted many of their values and perspectives on education; parents whose children are involved in the sort of extracurricular activities, such as figure skating or gymnastics, which make regular school hours almost impossible; or Internet-savvy techies from a younger generation who are convinced that, by using the Internet, they can educate their children better than the local public school.

There are also probably even more numerous and varied methods which parents apply in actually facilitating a homeschooling curriculum. Some parents employ very strict schedules while educating their children, even stricter than what they would be exposed to in classrooms of nearby schools. Others tend to weave their children's learning so completely into their family life that even certain basic skills can be gained from a trip to the store or helping with the family business.

Also, increasingly, homeschooling parents have banded together and hired teachers to come in from the outside and teach their children in small groups. In fact, this was exactly what a certain family who had sent their child to my school in Evanston, but who found that they would rather homeschool, did. They actually had formal lessons at one of their homes with a few other families, and although they called themselves a school and gave that school a name, it was still really just homeschooling for one important reason, which is that the instruction was still under the auspices of the children's parents.

This is an issue that needs addressing, this dynamic of homeschooling parents fusing themselves together as a group to provide formal instruction for their children. Increasingly, homeschooling parents are either connecting with each other in person to provide learning programs, almost as if they were a type of small school, or else connecting with each other on the Internet to initiate simultaneous online learning. In fact, there was a very well-organized group of homeschooling parents in Evanston, where my school was situated, from which parents either sent their children to our school to be educated or else on occasion left our school to pursue the homeschooling option.

What needs to be addressed is the issue of whether young people who are being homeschooled together in a small group or else are connecting to learn together online are achieving the same independence from home that those students who actually leave home for school every day initiate for themselves. This is important to consider because there may indeed be a certain dynamic relationship between independence and initiative.

It seems entirely possible that the more independent a young person becomes, the more initiative he will develop, an initiative that very likely extends well into his adult years. That is, it is simply human nature to be more adventurous with both one's life and learning if one has developed a certain independence inwardly from one's parents, and, in fact, that may indeed be a significant reason why, in the cases of many children, it is important for them to take that first step toward independence by leaving their home in order to attend school.

Indeed, there may even be a certain genetic, hereditary, even cross-cultural relationship between a young person growing his set of new, adult teeth and his need to journey farther out into his immediate environment in search of his growing independence. As scientists learn increasingly that early humans enjoyed the same long childhood that we modern humans do in order that the type of learning that leads to culture and complex society could be engendered, it seems entirely possible that this organic relationship between the growth of adult teeth and the need for increased independence may stem all the way from the advent of the first early humans, when the presence of one's adult teeth might have meant that one was ready to journey with one's parents in search of food on the African plain.

The point is that if it is indeed our nature to proceed with greater initiative the more independent we become, and if it is also the case that a number of homeschooling parents may be denying their children a certain amount of independence by not sending them off to school, then it follows that, in our present information age and connected global marketplace in which initiative is obviously a key to one's success as an adult, these same parents may on occasion be indirectly, although unintentionally, adversely affecting their children's futures.

Speaking from my own experience with young people who attended my school and who had been homeschooled until they were anywhere from eight to eleven years old, I can say that there was a distinct pattern of behavior that I observed in a number of these students. This was that quite a few of them possessed a certain degree of immaturity relative to their chronological peers. That is, both their relational skills with other young people in regard to their ability to deal with frustrating situations, and also the amount of responsibility they took for academic work for which they had agreed to be responsible were, often not what they needed to be.

This is certainly not to say that there were not students who had been previously homeschooled who were able to relate to their peers in a mature manner and who were also able to exhibit a significant degree of responsibility in regard to academic learning. In fact, there were a number of former homeschoolers who demonstrated a great deal of both of these qualities.

Yet, at the same time, there were enough students who had been previously taught at home whose behavior turned to extreme neediness when confronted with difficult interpersonal situations or whom I had to repeatedly nag or cajole in order for them to follow through on learning for which they had previously agreed to be responsible that I began to consider that there might indeed be a certain relationship between their homeschooling background and their often immature behavior.

For those homeschooling parents who might accept the supposition that it is often developmentally necessary for children to leave home for school in order to begin to establish their independence, but who would argue that by creating formalized educational programs with other homeschooling families, they are in effect allowing their children to do this, there might be something else for these parents to consider.

This would be simply that if these educational programs are entirely organized by and under the auspices of parents who are homeschooling their children, then those children are probably going to still feel that they are not actually leaving home to pursue learning activities with their peers for the simple reason that they know their parents are still the ones who are in control of these activities. Hence, it seems inevitable that they are going to feel, at least to a significant extent, that they are still in effect at home with them. To leave home inwardly at a certain age for the purpose of beginning the process of establishing one's independence is as much a state of mind as it is an actual physical reality.

There is also one other important psychological component that may affect young people who are being homeschooled. This is simply that because the messages that young people receive about themselves many times determine the people that they become, children who see most of their chronological peers go off to school when they do not may be receiving a certain indirect, subtle message about themselves that might affect their personal development.

This would of course be, particularly in the case of younger children, a message that might create certain doubts in the children's minds about their own maturity level and readiness to attend school. Even if their parents present them with the most reasoned, intelligent arguments for why they should be homeschooled when most other children are not, it still seems possible that at a more intuitive, even unconscious level, the children may begin to feel that they are somehow different. Of course, it is hard to know how one could prove or disprove such a dynamic statistically. It just seems that it might be something that parents who are inclined to homeschool their children should consider.

A number of parents are now also educating their children at home by enrolling them in online charter schools on the Internet, and many of these students are actually considered to be public school students, not homeschoolers, because their online schools are taxpayer-financed and even subject to federal testing requirements.

As one can probably imagine, a number of these schools have met with a certain amount of opposition from teachers, unions, and school boards because they divert state monies from the online students' home school district and also because it is often deemed unfair that some of these same state monies are used to pay for-profit companies who provide some of the online learning programs. In addition, there have been disputes over whether online schools who receive public funds can do so when it is primarily parents, not certified teachers, who are providing the personal instruction.

Yet, aside from these sort of legal and economic issues, the real question relative to online learning, particularly in regard to younger children, may be whether learning that is largely virtual is entirely healthy or appropriate. Despite the fact that there are many excellent online learning programs to be found on the Internet today, there are in fact significant differences between academic learning that is only virtual and that which is engendered in the context of a working relationship with an actual teacher and done in the company of other students.

One difference, of course, pertains to children assimilating new information and knowledge into already established cognitive structures and then, because of this, expanding those same structures as Piaget so brilliantly described. In terms of this basic, essential process of cognitive growth, it is entirely possible to believe that interaction with an actual teacher might make a significant difference. That is, although many online learning programs certainly provide clear, sequential feedback to students who are moving from one step in a particular learning sequence to the next, there is still not going to be the same essential give and take that a living, breathing teacher provides.

The key difference is obviously that an online learning program is only going to respond to a certain step in a particular learning sequence in a purely cognitive manner, while a real teacher's range of responses is going to be inherently much larger. For one thing, she is going to respond to the child as a whole person—that is, to any of his curiosities or questions which are related to the specific learning sequence—for no step in any particular learning progression exists in isolation from a whole range of related information, knowledge, and personal concerns.

For example, a child who is learning to tell time according to an online program is going to move from a particular skill, such as how to tell time according to the five-minute intervals on a clock, to a related skill, such as being able to tell time according to the single minutes between these intervals, in a manner that engages only his cognitive apprehension of these two specific, exclusive abilities. This means that, almost certainly, the online program is not going to deal with matters such as the conception of time itself or possibly the child's own unclear apprehension of causality or of the ideas of past, present, and future.

However, a child of a similar age who is working with an actual teacher to learn this skill is most likely going to employ a process of absorption that is quite different. For instance, after determining whether or not the child understands the concepts of duration (i.e., the idea that a certain event has a beginning and an end that can be measured by the movement of the hands on a clock) or of simultaneity (i.e., that two events can both happen at the exact moment at which the clock hands reach a particular position), the teacher might present lessons to him which are synonymous with what he will be able to assimilate given his understanding of the concepts of duration and simultaneity.

Therefore, as far as the development of this one particular skill, the ability to tell time, is concerned, there is a significant, rather fundamental difference between the online learning program and the instruction of a teacher which is not preprogrammed in any manner. This basic difference is that, in the case of instruction that comes from a living teacher, the teacher will be able to work with the student to strengthen certain cognitive structures so that he can assimilate new information into them more easily. However, as far as the online program, there is no realistic way to accomplish this, even with the assistance of an adult who may be supervising the online learning.

That is to say, an actual teacher has a whole range of choices available to her, stemming from a particular student's understanding and capacities, which can be used to acquaint a student with the ability to tell time, while a preprogrammed online program usually has only the next autonomous step in a preconceived sequence on which to depend. For instance, in the case of a child who grasps how two different events can occur at the same clock time but doesn't possess a clear idea of the concept of duration, the teacher could approach the learning situation in a way which stresses the latter.

For example, she could devise lessons in which the child matches familiar events in his life with pictures of pairs of clocks which represent different time intervals. Likewise, in acquainting a child with the concept of simultaneity as he learns to tell time, his teacher could have him match a number of events from his life which tend to occur at the same time with a specific time represented on a single clock.

The point is that with a living, involved teacher, there is a much greater chance that a process of assimilation and accommodation will occur, much as Piaget suggested, in which the teacher, through her personal experience with the learner, can devise certain activities that strengthen the student's capacity to absorb certain key concepts. However, in the case of a preprogrammed online learning sequence, the only real relation which the student has to what he is learning is in fact performing successfully at one step in the sequence so that he can move on to the next.

In other words, the process of how a student moves from the completion of one successful step in a sequence to the next (i.e., the development of his cognitive life) is not taken fully into account in the online program, only that he got to that next step. This is the real danger of any preprogrammed approach to learning; that it doesn't do as much to facilitate the student's actual intelligence as he learns as it might. It usually only teaches him how he can successfully move from one step in a particular learning progression to the next.

One possible long-term consequence of this is obviously that, although the acquisition of skills and information can of course be effectively engendered through online learning programs, certain important concepts on which these skills and information rest are never fully developed. Then, as a result of this incomplete development, the child's own evolving intelligence proceeds at a more superficial level than it otherwise might.

For instance, a student who learns basic mathematics essentially through an online program might indeed develop all of the relevant skills she might need to move on to the next level of her education, which would almost certainly be an upper-level elementary or middle-school math curriculum. However, if she isn't learning these skills through an open-ended, give-and-take, organic relationship which she has with an actual teacher, one has to question whether her capacity for genuine mathematical thought is indeed being facilitated.

Although she might comprehend all the requisite steps which are involved in performing each of the four basic mathematical operations, she might not fully understand concepts such as reversibility in relation to these operations or the one-to-one correspondence that is inherent between numbers and actual quantities in the real world. It seems that these are concepts which can only be fully developed if the young person is working with an adult to fully assimilate new ideas into cognitive structures which have previously formed.

Piaget has written of how after the age of seven or eight, the child performs operations upon his immediate environment which concern what Piaget refers to as transformations of reality by means of internalized actions that are grouped into coherent, reversible systems. This means essentially that the evolution of his mental life becomes increasingly a matter of developing the capacity to coordinate his own thinking with the external reality in which he finds himself.

For instance, Piaget uses the example of a four- or five-year-old who, although he could find his way between two places in close proximity with which he is familiar, would not be able to represent this same path using little three-dimensional cardboard objects. That is, he would be unable to mentally reconstruct the same path which he is successfully able to physically traverse. However, the child of seven or eight does begin to develop this capacity to mentally represent what he has absorbed previously solely through his actions.

Therefore, there is a great window of opportunity with school-age children to enhance the development of their intelligence through interactions with them which will allow them to more fully internalize the different aspects of their world. This means that because during this particular period of their lives they are in the very process of attempting to create a certain order within themselves that reflects the order of the world surrounding them, they are most likely going to either leave this period with a more focused, orderly mental life or with one that only superficially apprehends their immediate environment.

That is exactly why there is a certain danger inherent in the sort of preprogrammed learning which one finds in online learning programs. This is the danger that, particularly with younger children who have reached a certain critical window in regard to their cognitive development, students might not be able, without the sort of personal give and take that interactions with an actual teacher can engender, to facilitate within themselves a mental life which is as orderly as it might be and exists at as deep a level as it otherwise might.

Instead, what might occur when learning exists only as a series of steps which children traverse on the way to successfully completing a predetermined progression, not within the context of a full give-and-take relationship with a teacher, is that their intelligence might evolve at a level that is more superficial than it might otherwise be simply because the unique manner in which each child develops a certain order within himself is not being taken fully into account.

A child learning a particular skill or being acquainted with specific information or knowledge through an online program is going to essentially proceed through the same sequence in acquiring those skills, information, or knowledge that other students using the same program would. However, a teacher who teaches a child or even a group of children by endeavoring to teach them from the standpoint of what they are able to absorb at any particular time is often going to tailor her teaching according to the students' unique cognitive capabilities.

Children who are having difficulty acquiring certain skills or absorbing particular knowledge can have an approach developed by their teacher which begins with what they are not able to grasp cognitively so that these concepts can be strengthened before they become further acquainted with the particular subject matter. Certain activities, which are tailored to their specific needs, can be developed that strengthen those same cognitive capacities. These could

then be used to prepare the students to return to what they were originally endeavoring to learn, only this time with the requisite abilities
that will allow them to be successful.

However, a typical preprogrammed learning program, something
which was developed by others who didn't actually know the children before they came to the learning situation, will usually only
present the next step in a particular learning sequence to them, one
which they will either know initially how to successfully complete
or else will complete through essentially a series of trial-and-error
approaches which really do nothing to strengthen the particular cognitive capacities which may be preconditions for the type of learning
in which they are engaged.

So, although any number of online learning programs might be a
very good alternative for students whose previous cognitive development has prepared them to be successful at absorbing the details of a
particular learning sequence, there is a certain inherent danger for
students with undeveloped or incomplete cognitive capabilities—this
is that those students will not have their unique needs as learners addressed in the course of pursuing a specific online program.

The particular issues that have been considered in this chapter
have been addressed for a reason. This is to simply point out to parents, educators, and other interested parties who might think that
there is a better way to educate young people than in the typical self-
contained classroom, in which both initiative and curiosity are often
stifled, that online learning or homeschooling may not necessarily be
the best alternatives.

Certainly, there have been success stories with each. Yet, one has
to wonder if it might, in many cases, actually be more natural for
children who have reached a certain age to be schooled by adults
other than their parents in order that they might begin to assert their
independence, and for cognitive learning to transpire as completely
as it might, interactions with an actual teacher are often mandatory.

There is also one more significant issue in all this, which is the
personal dynamics inherent in a parent teaching his or her own chil-

dren. The concern here, of course, is whether that parent has the necessary distance to optimally instruct them. Teaching students in their formative years, particularly instruction that takes place on a one-to-one basis, in order to be fully effective, does indeed require a certain type of personal distance. This is the distance that allows someone instructing a young person to intelligently respond to his needs as a learner without reacting personally.

Needless to say, it is often very difficult for those who teach their own children to avoid responding to them out of either an inordinate amount of desire that they become effective learners or else out of the frustration that ensues when they don't. For of course, it is natural for a parent to be personally invested in their children's success and happiness in a manner that is almost entirely primal.

On the other hand, a teacher who is teaching someone else's child possesses none of the same primal anxieties that often ensue when there are difficulties in the young person's learning and personal development. She is able to stand back and simply focus on attempting to steer the student in the direction that she thinks will cause him to become a more effective learner, while a parent is much more at risk of succumbing to the tendency to react too personally to the child's successes and failures, something that will inevitably cloud her perceptions as a teacher.

During the time I founded and directed my school in Evanston, on several occasions, I hired parents whose children were enrolled in the school to also teach there. These were all good parents who possessed many admirable qualities as both parents and teachers. However, as teachers, none of them was really able, in my opinion, to effectively distance themselves from the needs of their own children enough to perceive the particular learning environment they were in with the sort of pristine eyes that effective teaching often requires.

The reason for this is both obvious and entirely natural: a parent's first concern is always going to be the needs of his or her own child. When that child grows needy in the context of any learning situation, then the entire educational environment is almost inevitably going to be viewed through the prism of those same needs. For instance, if a child comes into a learning environment with certain inadequacies in regard to a particular basic skill and the child's parent is teaching in that same environment, then it is going to be natural for that parent to feel that that same skill should be stressed more than it might need to be for all the students in the school.

Likewise, if another child is a bit of a loner who is uncomfortable spending a lot of time around other children and his mother, who also teaches in his particular classroom, supports his need for a certain amount of personal space, then that parent is probably going to want to restrict the amount of socialization that goes on between the children in the class while they are learning so that her own child doesn't feel so lonely. Once again, this is the sort of natural reaction that most parents who are in a similar situation would tend to have.

Therefore, this is something that a parent who decides to teach her children at home is going to need to focus a certain self-critical eye upon. That is, is she keeping her personal reactions to her children out of the particular path that she has carved out for them as learners? Or, even more importantly, does she really have the capacity to do so? Most likely, this is something that many parents simply wouldn't be able to do.

Once again, the reason why a discussion of some of the possible dangers inherent in both homeschooling and online learning have been included in a book that deals primarily with how to connect students more fully with the world of adult work and expertise is simply this: if certain parents believe that the best answer to how traditional schooling stifles both curiosity and initiative in young people is to simply teach one's children at home, then those same parents might consider that there could be a third alternative which facilitates curiosity and initiative but also engenders greater independence and also more fully realized cognitive development. This alternative is connections with the world of the professional who has a great deal of access to the very skills, information, and knowledge which young people will need in order to eventually be successful.

Of course, the issues underlying this entire discussion from both sides of the question are highly complex and difficult to address, to say the least—not just the possibility that there might be certain dangers lurking in the shadows when one decides to avoid the public schools by teaching one's children at home but also the issue of how to educate a large number of students in a self-contained classroom, with a certain amount of accountability, without the structure of their learning dampening their initiative and also causing them to become increasingly less curious about what they are studying.

Then, of course, there is the issue of how one might effectively link traditional schooling with the world of adult expertise in a manner that is organized enough that students actually are being educated by professionals through the sort of meaningful instruction that is followed up by teachers who effectively weave such instruction into their classroom studies. Certainly, if this is going to take place, then there are going to have to be not only significant structural changes but also even certain sacrifices on both ends.

A certain niche would have to be created in the world of busy professionals for this new function of educating young people by sharing one's expertise with them, and, as has been previously mentioned, the duties of the typical classroom teacher are likewise going to have to be expanded into the world of adult work by eliminating other, less important responsibilities.

There are obviously issues here that are going to take quite a bit of careful thought, planning, and organization. The sort of society which has been alluded to in this work is going have to be built carefully, piece by piece, in order that young people really can learn many of the skills, knowledge, and information that they will need to possess later by connecting with that same world of adult expertise that they will eventually enter.

Therefore, the chapter which follows is an attempt to address these organizational issues from an entirely practical standpoint. That is, it attempts to portray a more deschooled society in which adult experts share in the responsibility of educating young people by including them in certain aspects of their world which had previously been off limits.

To engender more meaningful, successful learning in our young people, and also to provide greater educational opportunity for students from certain socioeconomic communities who have previously been significantly marginalized, we are going to have to begin with a certain restructuring of our entire society, not just with changes which might take place in the structure of our schools.

Chapter Ten

Toward a Deschooled Society

By now, it probably seems obvious to most people reading this work that if schools in our society are going to connect themselves more fully to the world of adult work, then that world is going to need to make just as many structural changes as the systems of education with whom they are connecting. If teachers take it upon themselves to become conduits connecting their classroom learning to the world of adult expertise, and the latter is not set up to allow that to happen, then little will be gained.

For instance, if the powers that be in a certain school district are willing to change science curricula for their middle-school students so that a significant part of their learning can take place in the laboratories of local biologists, chemists, and physicists, but the colleges and research laboratories in the area haven't made the necessary scheduling changes that will allow lessons to proceed beyond the level of just another field trip to someone's workplace, then most likely, this attempt to connect schooling to the world of professional expertise will end in failure.

Or if other groups of students are scheduled to meet on a regular basis with different bankers and investors, but the businesspeople with whom the students are meeting significantly underestimate the students' general intelligence or capacity for mathematical or analytical thought because the amount of preparatory work needed to educate the professionals about the students' true capacities hasn't occurred, then these relationships between young people and professionals might easily not germinate into the sort of lessons that are truly educative.

So the question becomes, where do we start in attempting to motivate professionals to take on the added responsibility of becoming in effect educators, and, furthermore, what reason might they have to do so? In order to find the answer to this question, it might be wise to begin by looking at certain societies other than ours in order to ascertain what can be learned from how they raised and educated their children. If any of those societies were able to effectively weave the upbringing and education of those in their formative years into their worlds of commerce and/or basic survival, then potentially much might be learned from those endeavors.

The great education writer and media critic Neil Postman wrote of how, until the advent of the printing press at the beginning of the Renaissance, information was transmitted orally, and so because of this, young people had access to the very same information that adults did. Therefore, particularly because families lived in very small spaces, young people were in touch with all different aspects of adult experience.

However, with the invention of the printing press in the fifteenth century and the exponential increase in the number of books which followed, young people, unless they were able to read, no longer had access to the same information which adults did. That is, because information and knowledge were now transmitted primarily through the written word rather than orally, young people could no longer share in adult life to the same degree unless they could read at a certain level. Hence the school became the medium by which young people could be connected to adult society. As a result, childhood and adulthood became increasingly separate entities, the result being that children became significantly shut out of the world of adult skills and expertise.

Eventually, the school itself, which was originally designed to teach reading to children, expanded into a much larger institution which became more and more responsible for imparting the skills, knowledge, and information that young people formerly learned at home or in places such as shops and guilds. Ultimately, of course, the institution of school grew large enough that it became the primary organization that prepared young people for adult life. As it took on other functions in addition to simply teaching children to read, such as instructing them in many of the skills and much of the knowledge which formerly they might have had to acquire orally by living and working in the adult world, young people became increasingly separated from this world unless they regularly attended what has become the modern school.

In fact, until the end of the Middle Ages, the child was in fact seen as a small adult who mingled, worked, and even competed with mature adults. Yet, after that, children came to be increasingly viewed as separate types of human beings who would need to rely on schools to prepare them for entrance to the adult world from which they had now become permanently separated simply because they no longer had the same degree of access that the communication of information and knowledge orally had formerly given them.

Now, however, due to the Internet and World Wide Web, the entire situation, in a certain sense, is being run in reverse. That is, young people can now have access to any adult information, knowledge, or skills which they are able to both retrieve and comprehend. Consequently, they no longer have to so thoroughly depend on the school, as they once did, to connect them to adult society. All they have to do to be put in touch with the latest developments in science, the arts, the business world, or popular culture is to simply go online.

Of course, basic skills, in particular the essential skills of reading and writing, still have to be learned in order for young people to become fully connected to the society of which they are a part. Information and knowledge are obviously still imparted through the written word, even though programs available on cable television or YouTube assume some of this same function, although often at a highly superficial level. Yet, at the same time, it would seem that there is something that can be learned from looking at the social structures that allowed young people to be fully connected to adult society in medieval times when important particulars of the adult world were still transmitted orally.

One interesting concept that could possibly be carried over into today's world is simply the idea of schooling and education not being exclusively intended for those in their formative years. For example, the medieval school was an institution that was intended as a sort of technical school for the young and old alike. This means that people of all different ages were still being educated together. In fact, it really wasn't until the eighteenth century that the sort of age segregation which led to people of different ages being taught separately began to be implemented on a widespread basis.

Therefore, when the evolution of the modern school is studied more closely, this is one characteristic which might give us a clue as to how our present social structures might be changed in order to give young people a greater opportunity to be educated in the adult workplace—that is, to begin to organize learning in some fashion in a way that gives people of different ages a similar degree of access to the same subject areas.

This obviously wouldn't mean, of course, that children and adults are going to have the same capacity to comprehend particular information and knowledge. It simply means that there might be a way to organize learning in the society outside of school in a way that gives people of different ages the same opportunity to be connected to and be educated by the knowledge of the adult expert.

One significant development that might make this possible would be to simply institute a system of apprenticeships for young people similar to that which occurred centuries earlier. As was mentioned in an earlier chapter, Howard Gardner has suggested an apprentice system in which adult experts instruct young people in a concrete manner in regard to the different aspects of a craft, trade, or vocation in order to facilitate their cognitive development.

Building upon this idea, as was mentioned earlier, a system of sharing of certain functions in particular professions might be instituted, both to free up the adult expert to pursue more significant work and also for the purpose of educating those young people who are acquiring knowledge and information through their association with him or her. One example of this might be the use of high school students to check some of the statistical work with which a scientist working in his laboratory has to deal, with the high school students then training some of their younger middle-school counterparts in how to assist them. As both groups of students became involved, they would almost certainly become indirectly acquainted with much of the information, knowledge, and skills that the scientist employs to pursue his chosen life's work.

Another example might be those doing academic research, such as a history or sociology professor at a local university, being assisted in this by students who search the Web for the specific facts and details that she might need to complete her research. Again, as they engage in this sort of fact checking, the students would of course become acquainted with much of the information and knowledge that the scholar herself employs.

As these partnerships became developed more fully, information and knowledge might flow more freely between adults and young people without the need for them to first pass through all of the hierarchical stages that primary and secondary education implies. In addition, this free flow of knowledge might be implemented not only by schools partnering with experts but also by private agencies and individuals who are ready to do the necessary research and legwork that would facilitate meaningful connections between young people and the world of professional expertise.

That is, actual businesses could be created, run by individuals who operate separately from or even partner with either public education or private schooling. Their functions could include researching exactly which adult experts from the world of science, business, the law, the arts, or higher education would be open to sharing their expertise with young people; scheduling times at the experts' place of work where these connections could occur; and of course providing information to parents and young people living in a certain area which would allow them to become involved in these partnerships between professionals and students.

In fact, a private business might be at times even more effective than local schools in facilitating this flow of information and knowledge between adult experts and young people for a number of reasons. Among these would be: those working in the private organization would not feel threatened in any manner by young people being occasionally educated in the world of professional expertise rather than in the classroom in the way in which some administrators and teachers might initially feel themselves to be threatened, or those in the private business who serve as conduits would not be daunted or even discouraged by all of the bureaucratic scheduling and transportation concerns which would plague schools as they attempted to connect their students with the world of adult work.

Also, those in private organizations working toward creating a somewhat more deschooled society, because they would not be conditioned by working for years in the present educational system, might have a fresher, more unique perspective on the parameters of what learning in our society might become. Then, of course, as they learn from their experience in connecting young people to adult experts, this original vision could become exponentially enhanced.

In addition, these private individuals or businesses serving as conduits between young people and working professionals would be able to provide information concerning adult experts who are willing to share their expertise to different socioeconomic neighborhoods on a more equal basis than separate school districts, operating with differing amounts of resources, would be able to do. As a result of this, as was alluded to in an earlier chapter, greater equality of opportunity throughout the entire social spectrum of a particular geographic area could be facilitated.

For instance, in Chicago, young people living in the inner-city neighborhoods of North Lawndale or Englewood would have the same chance to become connected to adult experts that those students living in the much wealthier North Shore suburbs of Winnetka or Kenilworth would have if both groups had an equal degree of access to the information which would allow them to do this. If a private business charged a certain fee for providing this information to parents and young people, then perhaps some sort of federally funded program could be initiated which would defray the cost of this service for those who were not as easily able to avail themselves of it due to financial considerations.

At the same time, there is something that educators working in either public or private education could do that would be exclusive to their responsibilities. This is to implement curricula that are synonymous with the areas of professional expertise toward which those curricula lead, meaning that students are being adequately prepared in skills that are not only relevant to the changes that are constantly taking place in different areas of the contemporary workplace but also are in preparation for future partnerships with adult experts. Particularly this is true as our current age of immediate communication in an ever-expanding global marketplace affects the skills which are necessary to succeed in business, science, technology, or the arts.

In his classic book *The School and Society*, published during the first half of the twentieth century, John Dewey wrote of the isolation of the school from the world outside it. In particular, as anyone who is familiar with his writings knows, he addressed the issue of how young people are so often unable to apply what they are learning in school to their lives outside it or even to realize that there might be a significant connection between those two things.

In one especially poignant example, Dewey wrote of how a superintendent of schools in Moline, Illinois, located on the Mississippi River, once told him that every year he found that many of the children in his particular school district were surprised to learn that the Mississippi which they learned about in their textbooks had anything to do with the stream of water which actually flowed behind their homes.

Now, of course, this same stifling dynamic might be applied to certain students' inabilities to recognize that much of the basic algebra they learn is exactly what allows many of the games and programs on their computers to be written or that much of the music which found its way into this country during the slave trade some four hundred years ago has led toward much of the rap or hip-hop to which they listen on their iPods or that the discovery of electromagnetic waves during the latter part of the nineteenth century eventually led to the invention of their cell phones.

The significant point here is that if young people are in fact going to successfully partner with adult experts to expand their education, particularly as changes now occur rapidly in many different areas of professional life, those young people are most likely going to need to acquire certain skills and abilities. Otherwise, these partnerships will be unable to occur in the most optimal manner if students do not first develop the requisite skills that they need to allow them to comprehend what the adult expert is attempting to teach them.

For example, if a group of middle-school students was meeting regularly with a certain stock investor, and the investor was endeavoring to explain to them the concept of dollar cost averaging in investing (i.e., the idea that one way to be a successful investor is to invest the same amount of money overall for each time period regardless of the price of individual stocks), and the students didn't first understand the concept of a ratio, then it would be more difficult for them to understand what the investor was trying to teach them.

Or likewise, if another group of students was meeting with a medical researcher at his laboratory, and he was acquainting them with how he was attempting to inhibit the functions of certain proteins in the body so that they could then enhance the function of other proteins in a way that causes a person to become healthier, the students would be in a much better position to learn from the researcher if they first understood the basic idea of a function (i.e., how changes in one variable can simultaneously effect changes in a related variable).

Therefore, teaching students the skills they would need to have in order to fully comprehend the particular adult expertise with which they are becoming acquainted would remain very much the province of classroom teachers. In fact, if a system of familiarizing students with the knowledge, information, and skills of the professional were to work as optimally as it might, this identification of and then preparation in the skills that are necessary to make these partnerships as successful as they might potentially become would indeed be necessary.

This would mean, of course, that the educator would need to communicate regularly with the professional in order to discover just what skills students might need in order to genuinely learn from the latter. Hopefully, while this type of communication is ongoing, the school and the immediate society of which it is a part would begin to more fully merge into a new system of education in which the two become fused with each other.

In addition, if this were to transpire, then the idea of schools preparing their students for the adult world into which they are eventually headed would take on a new, more immediate meaning. That is, this preparation would begin to exist in the present for young people rather than being only held out to them as a path toward success in some distant future time, one that it is often hard for them to comprehend.

Once again, this integrated approach between schools and professional expertise might be an excellent chance to enhance educational opportunity for students who come of age in certain socioeconomic neighborhoods which do not provide them with the same advantages that young people in other neighborhoods might enjoy. This would particularly be true if the same lists of professionals willing to partner with students and the preparatory skills which could be taught them by their teachers were distributed equally among different neighborhoods.

Indeed, this is exactly the sort of advantageous service which a centralized bureaucracy such as the Department of Education or the office of the superintendent for large school districts could provide to families and young people that would be of genuine benefit. Then, everyone, regardless of the quality of their local school or the specific socioeconomic neighborhood in which they happen to live, could begin to have access to a similar level of educational opportunity in regard to the advanced learning which adult expertise would engender.

At the same time, it should be kept firmly in mind that the best way to foster advanced skills which are synonymous with specific adult expertise is to actually make a point of connecting students with adult workplaces on a regular basis. Otherwise, no matter how much work teachers do in their classrooms to give students the sort of skills that are necessary for them to learn from the professionals with whom they might partner, the impact on those young people's lives will be only minimal.

For this synthesis of schools with the workplaces of adults to occur on the sort of regular basis which would be necessary, two rather large impediments, which have been alluded to earlier, are obviously going to have to be overcome. One is the sort of intractable resistance by educators which is certain to occur among many of them when they realize that a certain amount of the educative process for which they had formerly been responsible is going to have to be shared with those working outside the schools. The other impediment, of course, is simply the inevitable unwillingness of many professionals working outside the school to give up some of their valuable work hours in order to take on this new educative function which they would be asked to assume.

Yet there is a certain argument that could be made to both the educators and the adult experts which might encourage them to participate in the sort of deschooled community which is the subject of this work. This is the idea of the development of a new type of student, one who is both more involved in his learning at school and who can also genuinely assist the professional if given the opportunity to do so on the way toward becoming more prepared for the adult world toward which he is headed.

Chapter Eleven

A New Student

Too often, both the initiative and curiosity of students are stifled when neither is given the opportunity to move fluidly beyond the classroom and schoolhouse door into the world outside where learning can be open-ended, unpredictable, and self-chosen. In addition, because we now live in an age in which young people can have immediate access, via the World Wide Web, to much of the same information and knowledge that adults have, even without attending school, the purposes of education need to be seriously reexamined, and they need to be reexamined in terms of the question of how students can become more engaged by their learning and in terms of how we might make access to the same level of learning more equitable across different socioeconomic boundaries.

In particular, because, with the advent of the Internet, we now live in a time similar to what occurred in the Middle Ages, when the invention of the printing press changed both the dynamics of learning and even the idea of what childhood was, we need to look seriously at the function of schooling itself: that is, what it can still do and what it is no longer best equipped to accomplish. It very well might be the case that we are looking today at the opportunity for a new type of student to be engendered, one who learns outside the age-old construct that most learning for young people necessarily takes place inside the local school.

Unfortunately, what often now determines how young people learn, despite much of the educational reform engendered during the past fifty years in Western societies, is the idea that learning is a process that is undertaken for some reason that is exterior to the learner himself. That is, it is done primarily to garner some result that is external to the actual learning process, such as a test score, grade, admission to the school of one's choice, or simply adult approval. In other words, despite much of the lip service given to this issue by progressive educators, seldom have dynamics such as initiative, curiosity, and interest been the primary factors which determine both student and teacher accountability.

The reason for this seems rather obvious. It is simply that the structure of contemporary schooling exists in a closed system in which successful learning and external validations of that learning, determined exclusively by educators, inevitably become synonymous. To put a finer point on things, learning by young people that takes place apart from the society in which they live, inside classrooms and schools that are separate from the community which surrounds them, cannot possibly be evaluated except in a manner that is almost entirely artificial.

The explanation for this is not so difficult to discover. It is simply that even though students in different classrooms might be successfully assimilating the information, knowledge, and skills that their teacher is providing them, there is little assurance that the students are likewise developing the practical capacity to use those knowledge and skills in the world in which they are relevant.

Particularly in today's age of immediate communication, in which the definition of what information is significant in different areas of endeavor changes so rapidly, a student who is becoming acquainted with a certain subject area, particularly if it involves mathematics, science, or computers, without comprehending how the skills and knowledge he may be acquiring are in fact used in the adult world outside of school, may well be already experiencing a serious disconnect with the society into which he is headed long before he becomes aware that this is occurring.

Like the students in Moline, Illinois, who were unable to associate the Mississippi River about which they were learning in their geography texts with the actual river which flowed near their homes, today's students, who aren't learning that the skills and knowledge they are acquiring in different subject areas are immediately applicable in the world of adult work which surrounds them, are learning in a closed system which does very little to enhance either their lives outside of school or their potential success in that world. Particularly this is true when so many students throughout the world *are* making those connections simply by retrieving the abundance of adult information, knowledge, and expertise that exists on the World Wide Web.

Thomas Friedman, in his now classic book *The World Is Flat*, writes of how each year, one thousand times more students in China enter the worldwide International Science and Engineering Fair sponsored annually by Intel than do American students. One of the reasons, of course, has to be the emphasis on science and computer technology that exists in countries such as China. Yet another reason, which may be even more significant, is that Chinese students might also be developing a firm grasp on the idea that their studies in school, particularly in mathematics and science, have immediate, real-world applications—hence their interest in demonstrating the development of these skills in venues such as large science fairs.

Therefore, there would seem to be one rather obvious answer to the often-asked question: how can we improve the mathematics and science skills of our students so that they're more on par with other countries such as China or Japan? This answer might be that we can develop those skills more in the world of adult work rather than to continue to exclusively develop them in the self-contained classroom. The same could also be said for those skills that involve the written word, particularly as literacy rates in our country continue to fall short of where they might be.

They key to all this occurring could be an approach which fuses initiative and accountability outside the contemporary self-contained classroom. This means simply that students in their formative years might be held more accountable for developing the initiative to use what they are learning inside their classrooms to more fully explore the world which exists outside the schoolhouse door, and, as was mentioned in the previous chapter, they could be assisted in this endeavor by educators working with adult experts to set up approaches in which specific academic skills are engendered which will prepare young people to optimally learn from the professionals with whom they are connecting.

With information and knowledge now so readily available on the Web, we really are now entering a new age just as profound as what occurred at the beginning of the Renaissance with the invention of the printing press or, as Neil Postman has elucidated so clearly in his writings, the one that came into existence in the nineteenth century with the invention of the telegraph, when information and knowledge could suddenly be transmitted electronically and instantaneously. Needless to say, this trend became exponentially enhanced by the invention of television, when young people suddenly had access to much of the same information to which formerly only adults had been privy.

However, it seems to be the case that many educators and social scientists haven't yet been able to absorb the implications of this new paradigm that is now transpiring in our current age, in which most everyone now has immediate, unfettered access to the same knowledge and information. Yes, of course, the Internet is now being fully integrated into the modern classroom as a source of learning. Yet the structure of school itself appears to be changing little in accordance with this profound development.

There can be little doubt that we now live in an age in which an enormous amount of the information, knowledge, and skills that were once only available to students in their local schools is now readily available to them on the Web. In accordance with this, we may well need a new type of school with new functions that become just as significant as its traditional function of being the basic provider of knowledge and skills. It is entirely possible that the emergence of the Internet is very much the equivalent of the invention of the printing press in the Middle Ages, when the idea of the modern school was conceived, yet our society and methods of education do not seem to have recognized the implications and profundity of this change.

More specifically, the skills and knowledge that young people will need in order to become more fully a part of the society into which they are headed are still being both engendered and evaluated apart from that society itself, even though all manner of information and knowledge now flows freely through our society. This occurs simply because our current mind set, carried over from previous historical periods, is that young people must necessarily and exclusively receive confirmation of certain knowledge and skill levels from their classroom teachers and administrators of their local school before they can actually set out to use those skills in the world outside of school—most of the time, only at a later stage of their lives.

Therefore, what's being proposed here is a new type of student, one whose actual learning occurs largely in the adult world toward which he is headed. The characteristics that would differentiate that student from those of the past would be: the pursuit of learning which is open-ended, unpredictable, and self-chosen rather than that which is essentially predetermined and chosen for one by others; learning which is stimulated more by adult experts working in their chosen field and, conversely, less exclusively by the traditional classroom teacher; an equal opportunity to learn from professionals regardless of one's socioeconomic background; and the development of greater initiative in students as they become more accountable for academic learning which takes place outside the schoolhouse door.

This, it would seem, is the type of student who will be more able to take advantage of an information age and global economy in which knowledge and skills are now being openly and horizontally transmitted around the globe between people from a multiplicity of different backgrounds and levels of expertise rather than only vertically and in a closed manner between a few experts and those who have been schooled to receive their particular expertise.

It is now possible for young people to contact and even learn from professionals working in different parts of the world through e-mail, text-messaging, MySpace, or YouTube. In fact, it would indeed be a wonderful development if some kind of national or worldwide directory of experts who would be willing to share their expertise with students could be made readily available. However, that still would be a rather pale imitation of students personally connecting with adult experts from various fields on a consistent basis.

One hundred years ago, the modern school had to change in order to become more relevant to a society that was moving rapidly away from an agrarian age toward an industrial age. Now, the exact same type of transformation is needed as we move increasingly into an information age in which the same knowledge is now readily available to everyone and also in which there is such fluidity between occupations, businesses, and even countries in our current global marketplace. As a consequence, the idea of learning taking place in a self-contained classroom that is essentially separate from the highly connected world of which it is a part is likely to become outmoded to the point where it is no longer necessary.

Therefore, what may be needed is a whole new model of imagining not only the modern school but also the definition of learning itself. That is, unless the modern school becomes a conduit to the community of which it is a part, the idea of schooling itself will continue to be less relevant to the idea of what it is to truly learn in our connected society. Should this transpire without new models to replace contemporary schooling, then it seems the same hands will continue to be wrung over the ever-recurring issues of ineffectiveness and lack of opportunity until the idea of educational reform itself may, out of frustration, significantly fade from our ongoing national discussion.

Bibliography

Ariès, Philippe. *Centuries of Childhood: A Social History of Family Life.* Translated by Robert Baldick. New York: Vintage Books, 1962.

Bennett, Alan. *The History Boys.* New York: Faber and Faber, 2006.

Bringuier, Jean Claude. *Conversations with Jean Piaget.* Translated by Basia M. Gulati. Chicago: University of Chicago Press, 1980.

Dennison, George. *The Lives of Children: The Story of the First Street School.* Reading, MA: Addison-Wesley, 1969.

Dewey, John. *Democracy and Education: An Introduction to the Philosophy of Education.* New York: Macmillan, 1916.

———. *The School and Society: Being Three Lectures by John Dewey Supplemented by a Statement of the University Elementary School.* Chicago: University of Chicago Press, 1899.

Dillon, Sam. "Online Schooling Grows, Setting off a Debate." *New York Times*, February 1, 2008.

Friedman, Thomas L. *The World Is Flat: A Brief History of the Twenty-First Century.* New York: Farrar, Straus, and Giroux, 2005.

Gardner, Howard. *The Unschooled Mind: How Children Think and How Schools Should Teach.* New York: Basic Books, 1991.

Hearn, Kelly. "160,000-Year-Old Child Suggests Modern Humans Got Early Start." *National Geographic News*, March 14, 2007. http://news.nationalgeographic.com/news/2007/03/070314-first-humans.html.

Holt, John. *How Children Fail.* New York: Dell Publishing, 1964.

———. *How Children Learn.* New York: Dell Publishing, 1967.

———. *Freedom and Beyond.* New York: E.P. Dutton, 1972.

Illich, Ivan. *Deschooling Society.* London: Calder and Boyars, 1974.

124   *Bibliography*

Kohl, Herbert. *I Won't Learn from You: And Other Thoughts on Creative Maladjustment*. New York: New Press, 1994.

Kohn, Alfie. *The Case against Standardized Testing: Raising the Scores, Ruining the Schools*. Portsmouth, NH: Heinemann, 2000.

Kozol, Jonathan. *Savage Inequalities: Children in America's Schools*. New York: Harper Collins, 1991.

———. *The Shame of the Nation: The Restoration of Apartheid Schooling in America*. New York: Crown Publishers, 2005.

Miller, Henry. *Tropic of Capricorn*. Paris: Obelisk Press, 1950.

Piaget, Jean. *The Child's Conception of Time*. Translated by A.J. Pomerans. New York: Basic Books, 1969.

Piaget, Jean, and Bärbel Inhelder. *The Psychology of the Child*. Translated by Helen Weaver. New York: Basic Books, 1969.

Postman, Neil. *The Disappearance of Childhood*. New York: Vintage Books, 1994.

Rogers, Carl. *Freedom to Learn for the 80s*. Columbus, OH: C.E. Merrill Publishing, 1983.

Schank, Roger. *Coloring outside the Lines: Raising a Smarter Kid by Breaking All the Rules*. New York: Harper Collins, 2000.

Singer, Dorothy G., and Tracy A. Revenson. *A Piaget Primer: How a Child Thinks*. New York: Plume, 1996.

About the Author

Lyn Lesch has been a classroom teacher for twenty-four years. After teaching in other schools for twelve years, he founded and directed The Children's School of Evanston, Illinois, a school for students ages six to fourteen, for another twelve years. The school received significant recognition from all of the major Chicago print and electronic media as a unique, innovative concept in education. He is the author of *Our Results-Driven, Testing Culture: How It Adversely Affects Students' Personal Experience* and *How to Prepare Students for the Information Age and Global Marketplace: Creative Learning in Action*, both books published by Rowman & Littlefield Education.